The Real Estate Investor's Guide to
CORPORATIONS, LLCs, AND ASSET PROTECTION ENTITIES

Also by Richard T. Williamson:

Selling Real Estate without Paying Taxes
Tax Secrets of Millionaire Real Estate Investors

The Real Estate Investor's Guide to CORPORATIONS, LLCs, AND ASSET PROTECTION ENTITIES

RICHARD T. WILLIAMSON, ESQ.

KAPLAN PUBLISHING

New York

This publication is designed to provide accurate and authoritative information in regard to the subject matter covered. It is sold with the understanding that the publisher is not engaged in rendering legal, accounting, or other professional service. If legal advice or other expert assistance is required, the services of a competent professional should be sought.

Vice President and Publisher: Maureen McMahon
Editorial Director: Jennifer Farthing
Acquisitions Editor: Michael Sprague
Production Editor: Julio Espin
Production Designer: Ivelisse Robles Marrero
Typesetter: Todd Bowman
Cover Designer: Rod Hernandez

© 2008 by Richard T. Williamson

Published by Kaplan Publishing, a division of Kaplan, Inc.
1 Liberty Plaza, 24th Floor
New York, NY 10006

All rights reserved. The text of this publication, or any part thereof, may not be reproduced in any manner whatsoever without written permission from the publisher.

Printed in the United States of America

May 2008
10 9 8 7 6 5 4 3 2 1

ISBN-13: 978-1-4277-9702-5

Kaplan Publishing books are available at special quantity discounts to use for sales promotions, employee premiums, or educational purposes. Please e-mail our Special Sales Department to order or for more information at *kaplanpublishing@kaplan.com* or write to Kaplan Publishing, 1 Liberty Plaza, 24th Floor, New York, NY 10006.

Dedication

This book is dedicated to
Michelle, Christina, and Rebecca

Contents

Preface xi
Acknowledgment xiii

1. **AN INTRODUCTION TO USING CORPORATIONS, LLCS, AND BUSINESS ENTITIES FOR REAL ESTATE INVESTMENTS 1**
   The Age of Litigation 1
      Assets + Liability = Lawsuits 2
      Too Many Aggressive Lawyers? 2
      Lawsuit-Happy Society? 3
   Overview of the Different Ways to Hold Property 7
      Individual Ownership 8
      General Partnerships 8
      Limited Partnerships 9
      Family Limited Partnerships 10
      Limited Liability Partnerships 11
      Limited Liability Limited Partnerships 12
      Chapter C Corporations 12
      Subchapter S Corporations 14
      Limited Liability Companies 15
      Series LLCs 16
      Living Trusts 17
      Irrevocable Trusts 18

2. **UNDERSTANDING HOW SEPARATE ENTITIES CAN PROTECT YOU—AND HOW THEY CAN'T 21**
   Liability Flow Basics 21
   The First Line of Defense 25

Setting Up Defense Barriers   28
Inside and Outside Liability   30
The "Keep It Simple" Approach   32
Grouping Properties   33
Separating Equity   35
Shifting Equity and Equity Stripping   36

3. FORCES THAT AFFECT YOUR ENTITY CHOICE   39

State Laws   40
Personal Business Needs   41
   Management Issues   41
   Profit Distributions   41
   Number and Type of Investors   42
   Succession Planning   42
Asset Protection, Limiting Liability, and Privacy   43
Formation Costs and Degree of Complexity   46
Yearly Cost and Administrative Burden   48
Getting the Right Advice   49

4. CHOOSING THE ENTITY TYPE: TAX CONSIDERATIONS   51

Income Taxes: Double-Taxed or Pass-Through Entity?   52
Dealer Property versus Investor Property   54
   Who Is a Property Dealer?   55
   Who Is a Property Investor?   55
   Why Does It Matter If You Are a Dealer or an Investor?   55
   Possible Ways to Avoid Being Labeled a Dealer   60
State Taxes   64
Estate Tax–Planning Considerations   64
Property Transfer Requirements and Pitfalls   67
Summary   69

5. CORPORATIONS   71

Why Subchapter S Corporations Are Better: Taxation Pros and Cons   71
Formalities of Formation   73
   Articles of Incorporation   73
   The Organizational Meeting   75

After the Organizational Meeting   78
The Resulting Hierarchy   80
Cardboard Corporations   81
Costs to Create and Operate   82
    Using an Attorney to Form Your Corporation   82
    Using Online Corporation Formation Services   84
    Incorporation Do-It-Yourself Books and Kits   87
    Yearly Tax Returns, State Fees, and Other Expected Fees   90
    Why You Should Consider Hiring an Agent for Service of Process   91
    Transferring Property into or out of a Corporation   92
Dealing with Government Agencies   93
Using Corporate Compliance Services   94
Piercing the Corporate Veil   94
Corporations Offer Little Protection from Outside Liabilities   97
Corporation FAQ   98

6. LIMITED LIABILITY COMPANIES (LLCS)   103
Have LLCs Replaced the Corporation?   104
Tax Differences and Considerations   105
Formalities of Formation   106
    The Articles of Organization   106
    The Operating Agreement   107
    Minutes and Appointing the LLC "Manager(s)"   108
    How Ownership Interests Are Defined and Issued   109
    What You Will Need to Conduct Business and Banking   109
Cost to Create and Operate an LLC   110
    Using an Attorney to Form Your LLC   110
    Online LLC Formation Services   112
    Do-It-Yourself Books, Kits, and Software   117
    Real Estate Deeding Process and Mortgage Pitfalls   117
    Agent for Service of Process Choices   119
Dealing with Government Agencies   121
Using Service Companies   122
Piercing the LLC Veil   122
Asset Protection and the Charging Order   124
Real Estate Investor LLC FAQs   128

7. THE SERIES LLC 133
A New Approach to LLCs 133
How a Series LLC Works 134
The LLC of the Future? 136
Formation Formalities 139
Cost to Create and Operate a Series LLC 140
Piercing the Veil and Charging Order Issues of the Series LLC 140
Series LLC Summary 141

8. LIMITED PARTNERSHIPS AND FAMILY LIMITED PARTNERSHIPS 143
Partnerships 144
Limited Partnerships 146
Family Limited Partnerships 147
    Asset Protection Benefits of Family Limited Partnerships 148
    Estate Tax Benefits of FLPs 152
    Family Limited Partnerships Targeted by the IRS 155

9. INCORPORATING IN ANOTHER STATE 161
Delaware 162
Nevada 164

10. DOMESTIC ASSET PROTECTION TRUSTS AND LAND TRUSTS 167
What Is an Asset Protection Trust? 167
    Is a DAPT Appropriate for Real Estate Investments? 169
    Problems with DAPTs 169
Land Trusts 171

11. OFFSHORE AND OTHER EXOTIC ASSET PROTECTION PLANNING 173

Appendix A: State Contact Information *181*
Appendix B: Sample Corporate Bylaws *187*
Appendix C: Sample Corporate Minutes *209*
Appendix D: Sample LLC Operating Agreement *217*
Index *223*

Preface

A TREMENDOUS AMOUNT of material has been written on the subject of asset protection. In fact, there is so much material and so many different points of view that it's very easy to get lost or overwhelmed. Seemingly "free" asset protection advice is everywhere and runs from basic, businesslike approaches all the way up to mind-boggling, multientity, multijurisdictional, supposedly "bulletproof" plans. Similarly, the credentials and expertise of the advisors out there run from the highly qualified to the highly questionable. With all the hype and marketing from seminars and the Internet, it has become very difficult to sort out fact from fiction. As a result, many people simply do nothing to protect their assets.

This book is intended to give you a starting place in thinking about asset protection and limiting liability. Its focus will be on business entities for real estate investors. The two types of real estate investment on which we will focus are (1) holding long-term investments like apartment buildings and other income property and (2) real estate businesses that do subdivisions, building, and rehabs. We will take a look at what types of entities are best suited for each of those activities, focusing on limiting any personal liability from the investment and then looking at how to protect the equity in those investments from potential liabilities arising elsewhere.

My intention is to keep the writing style very informal. I'm a lawyer, however, and sometimes that's not easy for me to do. Nevertheless, I'll try to explain things as I would to a client or a friend. I read a lot of asset protection books, and I'll be the first to say that the material can be so detail oriented that it gets tiresome very fast. My purpose in writing this book is to give you a starting place by writing in a way that is interesting as well as informative. What I hope you will get from this book is a basic understanding of the types of asset protection methods available to you as a real estate investor. However, understanding what can be done is not enough, so I hope this book also encourages you to implement some of these methods to protect your assets.

Acknowledgment

Christina Gentilini

A lot of hard work goes into writing a book. The effort takes hours upon hours of research, fact checking, designing graphics, creating tables, and organizing materials. And then there's the typing. It literally takes hundreds of hours to type a manuscript. And there are always those difficult chapters or sections that you end up typing, then rewording, then retyping again and again.

I was very fortunate in writing this book to have the help of my legal assistant (and daughter), Christina Gentilini. She did a lot of the legwork researchwise and was invaluable in helping to organize materials and keep me on track. Most importantly, she spent many hours over a computer keyboard converting dictation into a typed manuscript. She deserves credit for much of the physical work that was necessary to create this book. Without her help, it would probably still be a work in progress somewhere on my computer, and you would not be holding it in your hands.

1 An Introduction to Using Corporations, LLCs, and Business Entities for Real Estate Investments

The Age of Litigation

Approximately 70,000 lawsuits are filed in America every day. That's over 25 million lawsuits per year. We live in an age of litigation. No one knows exactly how we got to this point, but some of the conditions that surely contribute to the problem are thought to be

- an increase in the number of aggressive lawyers,
- the acceptance of lawsuits by the public,
- we've become a society of victims, and
- the disparity of wealth in this country.

It's also estimated that one of the fastest-growing segments of litigation is real estate and premises liability lawsuits. The fact is, if you own real estate, then you are a target for lawsuits. It's just that simple. Is it fair? No, but who says the world is fair? You can be sued by a tenant, by the guest of a tenant, or by a contractor working on your property; even the electric company's meter reader can sue you. You can be sued for something you did or for something you didn't do. You can be sued for things you knew about or for things you may not have known about but "should have" known about. You can be sued for the actions or inactions of other people whom you hire, like handymen, painters, or property managers. You can even be sued and held monetarily liable for criminal acts that occur on your property. All of this may sound a bit crazy, but it happens. If you own real estate, you better believe you *are* a target for lawsuits. How did we get to this point?

Assets + Liability = Lawsuits

Real estate investment has become more and more an integral part of retirement planning and wealth growth in American society. Just about every financially well-off person I have met derives a large part of his net worth from real estate investments. Unfortunately, while real estate has the potential to generate wealth, it also has the potential to generate liability. Moreover, owning multiple pieces of real estate creates multiple sources of potential liability. Anytime you combine wealth with the potential for generating liability, the result will likely be an increase in the number of lawsuits. And I'm not just talking about "Rockefeller-type" wealth—I'm talking about the average person who owns a home and has some equity built up in a rental duplex or maybe a piece of land that she inherited from a parent. It doesn't really matter who you are. If you own real estate, then you are a target for potential lawsuits, and you need to consider how to minimize your risk or contain the potential damage to your assets as a result of a lawsuit.

Too Many Aggressive Lawyers?

I can't even count the number of times I've heard someone say, "There are too many lawyers." Based on U.S. Department of Labor statistics available at the time of this writing, 735,000 persons were employed as lawyers, with 25 percent of them occupying government or corporate jobs. That means there are roughly 550,000 attorneys in private practice. Of those 550,000 attorneys, perhaps another 25 percent are transactional or planning attorneys and have nothing to do with lawsuits or litigation. That leaves about 400,000 lawyers. If you stop to consider that every lawsuit has a plaintiff's lawyer and a defendant's lawyer, you realize that about half of those 400,000 lawyers are out there to protect you. Now we are down to about 200,000 lawyers. Still too many, you say? Let's put this in perspective: those same U.S. Department of Labor statistics show us that there are 1.2 million accountants, 1.4 million engineers, 560,000 surgeons, and, amazingly, 2.6 million real estate agents.

So are there really too many aggressive lawyers? Maybe, but that's not the primary cause of the problem. With only a few exceptions, every attorney has to have a client to start a lawsuit. It does appear that lawyers have become more aggressive in pursuing real estate–related lawsuits. However, the litigation problem probably has more to do with society's perception of the legal system. Let's split society into two basic categories of "businesses" and "consumers." Consumers tend to use lawyers and lawsuits to "get paid for" some perceived wrong that they feel was done to them. Businesses, on the other hand, tend to use lawsuits to enforce rights that they believe are theirs. And, of course, whether a business or consumer initiates a lawsuit, the responding party must also hire a lawyer. The result is that for every lawsuit filed, usually at least two lawyers are getting (or trying to get) paid.

Some of those lawyers—generally those who represent the claimants/plaintiffs—make money on a contingency fee basis, which means that they only get paid by settling or winning lawsuits. The more lawsuits and the higher the dollar-value per lawsuit, the more money the lawyer makes. Lawyers need to make a living like everyone else, so it should be no surprise that some lawyers might seem overly aggressive in pursuing their client's "right" to be compensated for any perceived injury.

Lawsuit-Happy Society?

Every day we are reminded that we live in a litigious society. How many law-related shows are on TV right now? There seem to be dozens, and they're wildly successful. *Judge Judy* and *The People's Court* have become household names. And what about the news media? They always like an eye-catching headline. Who hasn't heard about the lady who sued McDonald's for $3 million because the coffee was too hot? And what about the story of the man who, while burglarizing a property, falls through a skylight and sues the property owner for a broken arm? Then there are daytime television advertisements from lawyers themselves. For many years in Los Angeles, advertisements and billboards throughout the city featured a client who says something like, "My attorney Harry Harper got me $2.1 million (names changed to protect the innocent)." In every large city across the nation, buses and taxis are plastered with advertisements for personal injury lawyers. As a society, we really are flooded with signs, billboards, and advertisements promoting lawsuits. So do we live in a sue-happy society? You bet we do.

The focus of this book is protecting your assets from lawsuits that might arise from owning real estate or engaging in real estate investments. We're going to look at how to create barriers that will stop a lawsuit on one property from affecting another property or other assets of the property owner. Such an understanding is absolutely essential in the litigious society I've just described. Many everyday people own real estate for years only to find all of their equity and their homes at risk because of a lawsuit. Here are two examples of these hypothetical scenarios:

Example 1:
Bob and Mary own a four-unit rental property in a reasonably good rental area of town. The property is worth about $600,000 and has a (refinanced) mortgage of approximately $400,000. They hold the property in their own name as husband-and-wife as joint tenants. They bought it many years ago and have managed it themselves the whole time. They try to take good care of the property and have always been diligent about making repairs.

Likewise, they're fairly careful about whom they rent the property to and try to maintain good relationships with all their tenants.

Recently, one of the tenants had a friend over for a visit. As the visitor left the apartment and walked down the driveway to her car, a man stepped out of a dark area and robbed her. During the robbery, the visitor was shot and killed. The family of the victim has served Bob and Mary with a premises liability and negligent security lawsuit for $5 million. Bob and Mary have landlord insurance on the property, but it will only cover them for a few hundred thousand dollars per incident. If the lawsuit is successful, the insurance will be completely used up, and Bob and Mary will lose whatever equity they have in the four-unit rental property and face the very depressing prospect that their home and life savings may be lost.

Example 2:
Eighty-year-old Doris owns three small houses by the beach. The houses are side-by-side, and she lives in one and rents out the other two. She's lived in this small beachfront community for about 50 years. Over that time, the houses have become very valuable.

She rented one of the houses to a seemingly nice couple who had relocated from another area. After they moved in, Doris noticed that they never opened their windows or blinds. Living in an area where most people appreciated the cool ocean breezes, she thought it was a little odd that they would keep the house closed up tight, but she didn't make anything of it. Soon, however, she noticed that there appeared to be an unusual amount of condensation forming on the interior of the windows. When she mentioned it to the tenants, they became somewhat abrasive and implied that she should mind her own business.

A few days later, she received a notice from the city informing her that the tenants had filed a formal complaint alleging substandard living conditions on the property. A city inspector came out to the property and noted a few very minor code violations, which she immediately corrected. Understandably, Doris was unhappy and decided that she no longer wanted to rent to the couple. Following her obligation as a landlord, she gave them a 30-day notice to move. At the end of 30 days, the tenants failed to move out. Doris hired a lawyer and started the legal process necessary for an eviction. After many delays caused by the tenants, her day in court finally came. The tenants showed up and alleged that they were being wrongfully evicted in retaliation for notifying the city of the substandard conditions. Seeing that there was a formal complaint filed and violations were found, the judge had no choice but to dismiss the eviction case.

Doris's health had been declining, and she passed away about four months later, leaving all three properties to her only son. Within two weeks of her passing, the son was served with a lawsuit against her estate from the tenants. The lawsuit alleged that she had maintained the property in such a way as to foster the growth of mold and that both of them were suffering severe respiratory difficulty as a result.

Obviously, the second example appears to be a situation in which a predator sees an opportunity to use the legal system to steal this woman's property. Unfortunately, these types of people exist. Doris had never seen a reason to consider taking action to protect her assets. Such measures might not have stopped the attack of these unscrupulous people, but they would have limited the amount of damage. When trouble comes, how you hold property and what types of asset protection precautions you've taken will make all the difference in how much damage can be done. The time to do that planning is before trouble arrives.

If you think the story of Doris seems a little far-fetched, take a look at the following actual lawsuit:

Jury Award: $1,274,150
A mother and her three daughters alleged injuries due to mold exposure in their rented condominium. (California, May 2004)

Overview of the Different Ways to Hold Property

There are many possible ways to take title to real estate. Most people hold real estate investments personally, as an individual owner or a married couple, in their own name; for example, "John and Jane Doe, husband and wife as joint tenants." This is the easiest way to own property but also the most perilous. The other choice is to own the property in some type of entity. In this section, we're going to give you an overview of some of the more common entities that might be used for real estate. The term *entity* as used in this book is defined as follows:

Entity:
Something that has a distinct legal identity, separate from its owners, and is capable of independently owning property

Corporations, limited partnerships, limited liability companies (LLCs), and trusts are all examples of entities that can own real estate. It's also possible to have multiple-entity ownership or entity-within-an-entity ownership. For example, some investors have a corporation or a trust that owns interests in an LLC that, in turn, holds title to the property. The possible combinations are as varied as the imagination. A good starting place to understand them is an overview of some of the different types of entities that are commonly used to hold real estate.

Individual Ownership

Individual ownership is actually not an entity at all, but we start here because probably 90 percent of the investment property owned in America is titled to individuals. An "individual" could be a single person, a married couple, or people who have pooled their money to purchase the property. Individual ownership is the easiest and most straightforward, but also the riskiest, way to own investment real estate.

Pros:
- Has no startup costs.
- Owner maintains 100 percent control.
- Owner receives 100 percent of income.
- Is the simplest of all types of investment property ownership.

Cons:
- Unlimited liability
- No asset protection

General Partnerships

Any time two or more individuals come together for a business purpose, including the ownership of investment property, the default business type is a *partnership*. If there is no formal partnership agreement limiting the liability of any of the partners, then the partnership type is a *general partnership*. Some general partnerships start out with a formalized partnership agreement, but for the most part, general partnerships are usually just two or more people who agree to carry on an enterprise or investment by combining funds, skill, and effort and then to share in its profit. In the general partnership, all partners are considered as managing the partnership and are personally liable, both jointly and severally, for its debts.

Pros:
- Equal rights and responsibilities for the partners
- Flexible and easy to start up
- A pass-through entity for tax purposes

Cons:
- All partners have unlimited personal liability for debts and obligations of the partnership.
- Shared decisions can lead to disagreements.
- Offers no asset protection from creditors of the individual partners.
- A death of one of the partners may force a liquidation of the assets.

Limited Partnerships

A limited partnership is a formalized, structured partnership of two or more people in which one or more of the partners becomes the *general partner* and one or more of the partners become a subset called *limited partners*. The intention is to allow some of the partners to have little or no exposure to liability for debts of the partnership. Limited partners are generally people who invest money in the partnership but have no active management of the business or investment. At least one (or more) of the partners must take an active management of the partnership, and that person, the general partner, is the only one personally at risk if the investment goes bad or the partnership is sued. Generally, a limited partner's exposure to liability is limited to the amount that person has contributed to the venture or investment.

Pros:
- The limited partners' liability is tied only to their investment in the business.
- Is flexible and easy to start up.

- Provides asset protection from the debts of individual limited partners.
- Is a pass-through entity for tax purposes.

Cons:
- General partner(s) have full unlimited liability.
- Limited partners may not participate in management.
- Requires a formalized partnership agreement and must be registered to do business in the state.
- Pays additional annual tax in some states.

Family Limited Partnerships

As the name implies, this entity is a limited partnership that is generally owned by a number of family members. A family limited partnership, commonly abbreviated as FLP or called a *flip*, operates the same way as any other limited partnership. Family limited partnerships became very popular in estate tax planning, because they gave aging parents the ability to move wealth from one generation to another. The parents would generally pass (gift) to their children a percentage of the ownership of the FLP, thereby removing it from their taxable estate while still retaining full control of the FLP-owned business or real estate investment. The family limited partnership became the standard of practice and preferred method of both protecting the assets and planning for estate tax reduction. FLPs are still very popular in family-owned businesses for estate tax planning.

Pros:
- The family limited partners' liability is tied only to their ownership of the investment or the business.
- Allows for planned wealth transfers between generations while still providing asset protection.

- Can help reduce estate taxes.
- Is a pass-through entity for tax purposes.

Cons:

- Requires advanced planning involving more attorney and accountant involvement.
- Requires a formalized partnership agreement and must be registered to do business in the state.
- Has additional annual tax in some states.

Limited Liability Partnerships

Limited liability partnerships, or LLPs, are similar to limited partnerships except that all partners have limited liability akin to that of corporation stockholders and all retain the right to manage the business directly. LLPs are not allowed in all states, and some states restrict their use to professional businesses. For example, LLPs are common for professionals like lawyers, doctors, and accountants. LLPs can be used to hold property, but generally speaking, they are better suited for ongoing professional partnerships.

Pros:

- All partners receive limited liability protection.
- All partners may participate in the management and decide structure and distributions.
- Is a pass-through entity for tax purposes.

Cons:

- Some states limit the types of people who can form an LLP.
- Requires a formalized structure and state registration.
- Some states require payment of an annual tax.

TABLE 1.1 *Summary of Partnership Types*

	General Partnership	Limited Partnership	Limited Liability Partnership	Limited Liability Limited Partnership
Role of the Partners	Equal rights and responsibilities.	General partner(s) with control; limited partner(s) with very little control.	Equal rights and responsibilities.	General partner(s) with control; limited partner(s) with very little control.
Liability Protection	No protection for anyone. All partners are personally liable for debts of business.	Liability protection for limited partner; no protection for general partner. General partner is personally liable for debts of business.	Liability protection for all partners.	Liability protection for all partners, whether general or limited.

Limited Liability Limited Partnerships

If all the *L*s here are confusing you, you're not alone. The limited liability limited partnership, or LLLP, is similar to the basic limited partnership; there is a designation of general partners, who control the business, and limited partners, who are primarily as investors. The difference between the limited partnership and the LLLP is that even general partners receive some liability protection in the LLLP. Also, an LLLP is not restricted to certain professionals as is the LLP. This makes its use more widely available for the real estate investor, except that LLLPs are not well established and are not allowed in some states.

Pros:
- Allows for liability protection for all partners, whether general or limited.
- Is not restricted to professional services.
- Is a pass-through entity for tax purposes.
- Is a flexible form of business.

Cons:
- Too new to have an established track record for protecting general partners from liability.
- Is not available in all states.
- Some states require payment of an annual tax.

Table 1.1 summarizes the features of each kind of partnership.

Chapter C Corporations

The most commonly known business entity is the *corporation*. Corporations have been around for hundreds of years. They are created by filing articles of incorporation with the state in which the corporation is being formed. Corporations fall into two basic categories: *public corporations* and *close corporations*. The difference between the two is simply whether the corporation's stock is publicly traded or privately owned. A corporation is an independent entity that has the legal ability to hold property and conduct business independently of its shareholders. The shareholders are entitled to the profits of the corporation but are completely insulated from debts and judgments against it. Once formed, a corporation is controlled by its directors and run by its appointed officers.

The Chapter C corporation (usually just called a C corporation) is the standard corporation you would think of as having stock shares that are traded on the New York Stock Exchange or the NASDAQ. Although it is the best-known entity, the C corporation has one distinct disadvantage: profits are taxed twice. The corporation itself has to file a tax return and pay corporate taxes on its income. After those taxes are paid, the corporation distributes the remaining profits to its shareholders, who individually have to claim these dividends and pay taxes on them yet again. C corporations are generally not considered appropriate for holding real estate investments (see S corporations on the next page).

Pros:
- Provides proven liability and asset protection for shareholders (owners).
- C corporations do not dissolve when an owner leaves, retires, dies, or is otherwise no longer involved.
- Some costs and expenses not deductible by other entity types are deductible.

Cons:
- Are separately taxed at the corporate level as well as the shareholder level.
- Must file and register with the state, making them more complicated to start up.
- Must create bylaws and hold stockholder meetings, write out minutes, etc., producing a greater administrative burden.
- Are more costly to set up and maintain.
- Some states require payment of an annual tax.

Subchapter S Corporations

The subchapter S corporation has all of the same formality, formation, and asset protections of a C corporation except that an election (subchapter S election) is made to have the profits of the corporation passed through directly to the shareholders. There are limits to the number and type of shareholders who can own subchapter S corporate stock. However, these restrictions usually have very little impact on the needs of the small business owner. As such, the subchapter S corporation is the standard for small business corporations.

Pros:
- Provides reliable structure and limited liability for shareholders.
- Provides some asset protection from individual shareholder creditors.

- Taxation passes through to the shareholders (no taxation at the corporate level).
- S corporations do not dissolve when an owner leaves, retires, dies, or is otherwise no longer involved.

Cons:
- Must file and register with the state, making them more complicated to start up.
- Must create bylaws and hold stockholder meetings, write out minutes, etc., producing a greater administrative burden.
- Some states require payment of an annual tax.

Limited Liability Companies

Limited liability companies, commonly referred to LLCs, are a relatively new business entity type. In the past 20 years, LLCs have grown dramatically in popularity. Many people mistakenly refer to LLCs as "LLPs" or as "limited liability corporations." LLCs are neither partnerships nor corporations. They do, however, combine the best features and best tax aspects of each of those entities. Like corporations, LLCs have well-established liability-limiting characteristics without the rigorous formal requirements of having directors and officers and annual meetings. An LLC is run by a designated managing member or collectively by all members and is controlled by an operating agreement created at the time of formation. The tax treatment of an LLC is similar to that of a partnership in its simplicity. Like a corporation, the filing of articles forms an LLC, but instead of articles of incorporation, an LLC has *articles of organization.*

Pros:
- Owners/members of the LLC are not personally liable for the debts of the business.
- Provides asset protection from creditors of members (owners).

- Can be taxed as a partnership, sole proprietorship, or corporation depending on the number of members and if the business elects to be treated as a corporation.
- More flexible than an S corporation in type and number of owners.
- Formation and ongoing administration formalities are less burdensome than those of an S corporation.

Cons:
- Is taxed at the corporate rate in some states.
- Still requires some degree of formality and ongoing administrative expenses.
- Some states require payment of an annual tax.

Series LLCs

The series LLC is a relatively new business entity not recognized in every state. The series LLC creates a master entity that is made up of, or contains, multiple business ventures or properties. Each of the separate ventures or properties makes up a *cell* or *series* of the LLC and is independent of the others. The idea is that one limited liability company can own a number of ventures or properties in cells, keeping them protected from each other for liability purposes. The series LLC is ideally suited for holding multiple pieces of investment real estate. However, it is not widely used because it is so new and how different states will interpret its internal liability protections is still open to question. Likewise, there is some question as to how the IRS will treat the tax considerations of series LLCs.

Pros:
- Has the ability to hold many properties in separate cells under one master LLC.
- Conceptually, only one master tax return must be filed instead of one for each LLC cell.

- Owners/members are not personally liable for the debts of the business.
- Each cell is shielded from any other cell's liability.

Cons:
- Only a few states allow the formation of a series LLC.
- Asset protection between the cells is not well established.
- Some states (e.g., California) that do not have series LLC legislation require you to file separate tax returns for each cell or series.
- Some states require payment of an annual tax.

Living Trusts

A living trust is known by a variety of names. To lawyers, a living trust is called an *inter vivos trust,* but common names also include *revocable trust, family trust,* and *probate avoidance trust.* A living trust is not designed to protect assets; it is designed for succession planning and probate avoidance. Living trusts are mentioned here only because a widespread misconception persists about their role in asset protection. *A living trust offers no protection whatsoever from creditors, so it is never a consideration for asset protection purposes.* Nevertheless, if you own real estate, you should have a living trust. They will not keep your assets safe from creditors, but when you pass away, a living trust will keep your assets out of the probate court system. Moreover, a living trust will work in conjunction with whatever type of asset protection entities you choose to use in your situation.

Pros:
- Efficient probate avoidance planning
- Efficient in capacity planning
- Inexpensive and easy to implement
- A "disregarded entity" for tax filing purposes

Cons:
- Provides no asset protection for trust assets.
- Provides no limited liability from trust assets.

Irrevocable Trusts

There are a whole host of different irrevocable trusts. To understand irrevocable trusts, you have to start with the basic definition of a trust. The definition of a trust is surprisingly like the definition of a corporation or a business entity. A *trust* is simply a contractually formed legal entity designed and created to hold property. The trust document itself is a set of instructions for what to do with the property transferred to the trust. With this wide-open definition, you can see that irrevocable trusts can be used for many different purposes by simply varying the instructions contained in the trust document. The main difference between an *irrevocable trust* and a *living trust* is whether the creator of the trust, or *grantor*, has the ability to amend and revoke the trust document or its provisions. All living trusts are amendable and revocable at any time for any reason. Irrevocable trusts, as the name implies, cannot be changed or revoked.

Pros:
- Is well suited for a variety of uses.
- Usually qualifies for pass-through tax treatment.
- Provides privacy.
- Is moderately inexpensive and easy to implement.

Cons:
- Is very difficult to change once implemented.
- Raises potential tax issues in certain uses.
- May need separate tax ID and annual tax returns.

There are additional entity types, and new ones seem to emerge every few years. Moreover, many of these entity types can be combined with others to create hybrids, entities within entities, or entities that own entities. Despite this complexity, we must not lose sight of what we're trying to accomplish: limited personal liability and asset protection. In this book, we will take a closer look at the most useful of these entity types, but before we do so, we need to understand the basics of how liabilities can flow from a real estate investment and to a real estate investment. Once we understand what we're trying to shield against, then we can understand how separate entities can offer protection—and how they can't.

2 Understanding How Separate Entities Can Protect You— and How They Can't

Liability Flow Basics

Many of my clients don't really understand the concept of asset protection. In a typical scenario, a client has a couple of rental properties, a primary residence, and perhaps a business of some type. The client often asks me, "Should I just form a corporation and put everything in it to protect me?" This question reveals a common misunderstanding of how asset protection works and how liability "flows" either from a person or to a person. In fact, one corporation or any other type of asset protection entity is useless if it contains all of the assets. The old saying "Don't put all your eggs in one basket" is especially relevant in asset protection.

The concept of liability flow shows us that not only does liability flow from a person and to a person, it also can flow from an investment and to an investment. In Figure 2.1, you can see that liability (shown by arrows) flows from the investments to you, from you to the investments, and also from you to your other personal assets.

The goal of asset protection planning is to use commonsense methods to disrupt the flow of liability. Let's start with the idea that liability flows from an

FIGURE 2.1 *Liability Flows from You and to You*

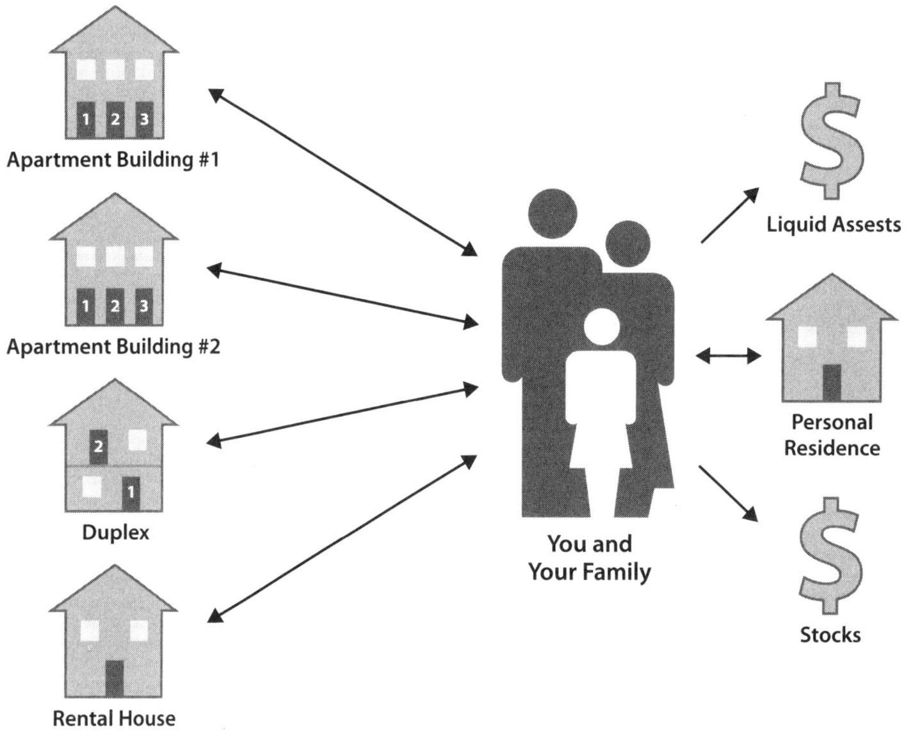

individual or to an individual. Liability flowing from an individual means that individual did something or caused some situation that incurred liability. Let's look at an example:

> While driving your car, you rear-end another car. If the accident was your fault, you are personally liable, and damages from that accident will be your responsibility. That liability now exposes all of your assets to the risk of loss from a lawsuit.

In Figure 2.1, the flow of liability in the above example is represented by all the arrows that point away from you to all of your assets.

On the other hand, liability that flows to an investor or individual is usually from something they own rather than something they did. In Figure 2.1, this flow is represented by the arrows pointing from your investments to you. Here's an example:

> You own a duplex in which one tenant owns a potentially dangerous dog. You are aware of the animal and know that the tenants who own the dog share a backyard with another tenant on the property who has small children. If the dog injures one of the children, logically, the first responsibility goes to the dog owner. However, if the dog-owning tenant has very little money or few assets, the lawyer will look for other people to sue to get damages or compensation for the injured child. So to whom does the lawyer turn next? The landlord.
>
> This is where the first line of asset protection comes in: insurance. The landlord in our example likely has insurance, so the insurance company gets involved. However, depending on the level of damages, the amount of insurance, and the severity of the injuries to the child, the insurance may not cover all of the damages. The liability then falls on the owner of the property.

The flow of liability in our example is as follows:

1. Look to the tenant who owns the dog. This is a dead end in most cases. Tenants likely have no insurance, and they usually have no other real estate or other assets. A lawyer is generally not going to try to garnish their wages or anything like that to collect on the judgment; rather, attorneys will look past the tenant to deeper pockets, which leads us to
2. the property insurance company. But again, there might be a limit to the amount of available insurance. So then the next deep pocket is

3. the owner of the property. You may not think that a dog bite on your property is your responsibility, but if the lawyers can show that you were aware of the dog, they will allege that you allowed a dangerous condition to exist on your property.

It is important to know the series of thoughts that go through a lawyer's head when assessing liability. The most important is, "Is there someplace or someone to recover funds from if we win this lawsuit?" Let's call this a "deep-pockets assessment." The lawyer will look to the tenant first, the insurance company second, and the property owner third. As the lawyer looks to the owner, he is actually breaking down the owner's assets into different categories. Say the owner in our example above has a duplex, a house, and a couple of other properties. If the lawyer finds a significant amount of equity or assets, then it is more likely that he will be able to recover damages if the lawsuit prevails. Of course, in the world of litigation, the lawyer would prefer to have a sufficient insurance policy to go after, but if the damages are high enough, they will look at equity in the property and the property owner's other assets as well.

With that said, a deep-pockets assessment usually categorizes property investors in one of several ways. The first would be just the everyday investor, who maybe owns a couple of rental properties in which she has equity, a home, and maybe some other assorted assets. All of the assets are in the investor's own name and easily identifiable. All of these assets could be at risk in a lawsuit. The same risk exists for investors who think that they should put all of their assets into one entity. This is self-defeating, because now all of the assets are clumped together and are all subject to every other asset's liability. These investors are not protecting any part (property, business, etc.) from any of the other parts (other properties, their own personal residence, etc.).

The second category of property owner in terms of a deep-pockets assessment is one who has put some type of asset protection plan in place. This person may have many other assets, but the property where the dog attack occurred has been placed in some type of separate entity. This means that the liability flow cannot get back to the investor. If the right entity protections are in place, then the only asset the lawyer can look to is the equity of the property where the event occurred. For example, if the property where the dog attack occurred has an 80 percent loan-to-value mortgage in place, then the mortgagor is a secured creditor and already has a claim to the equity of that property or at least to the repayment of their note. This gives the attorney very little to go after. This in turn tempers the lawyer's aggressiveness; with little equity to go after, the lawsuit is not as worthwhile as one with a potentially bigger payoff.

It is important to know how the liability will flow to you as a property owner. You will not be able to prevent the flow from going from the tenant to the insurance company and, if there is not enough coverage, to you. But you can stop the liability from threatening *all* of your assets. We will talk much more about this later. First, however, it's important to know some things about insurance.

The First Line of Defense

Once you understand how liability flows to an individual and from an individual, then it becomes important to understand how you can limit liability so that it flows only in limited circumstances or is completely shielded from your other assets. The first line of defense in any kind of asset protection is insurance. In a perfect world, you could always buy insurance that would shield your other assets from the liabilities of your real estate investments.

For investor properties, there is landlord insurance. Landlord insurance has a variety of amounts for which you can insure and a long list of exemptions that are not covered. To avoid feeling a false sense of security, you need to understand the insurance you are buying and what it covers. The full range of possible landlord insurance coverage options is beyond the scope of this book, so we will focus on some of the basics.

The amount of insurance that one buys is really up to the individual investor and his level of discomfort or, to put it more bluntly, his level of paranoia. I advise my clients to buy as much insurance as is needed to let them sleep comfortably thinking that they have adequately protected their property. (I do the same myself.) It is certainly possible to go overboard. For example, buying a $5 million liability policy on a duplex is probably overkill. It would be very expensive, and it is so far beyond the realistic risk level that only the truly paranoid person buys this much insurance. Having said that, there are truly paranoid people out there, and if you're one of them, insurance companies will be happy to take your money.

How much insurance is enough? There are a few factors to consider. These include the size of the property, the likelihood of a liability-generating event, and the likelihood of more than one liability-generating event in a year. A single-family home used as a rental house is considered a pretty low risk. On the other end of the spectrum would be a 16-unit apartment complex that is used as interim housing for transients or something along those lines. Interim housing for transients isn't exactly common, but even a 16-unit apartment that's all one-bedroom apartments or singles can be a high liability risk. As such, more significant consideration should be given to the amount of insurance needed.

In the case of a single-family rental home with low liability risk, adequate insurance might be a $100,000/$300,000 policy, meaning the maximum coverage per loss is $100,000 and the maximum aggregate coverage per year is $300,000. (Some policies don't have an aggregate limit.) On the other hand, in a building with a larger number of tenants, lawsuits will be more likely. In those situations, a $1 million/$2 million policy (or higher) might be more appropriate.

Also important in disrupting the flow of liability is knowing not only how much insurance to get but also what type. There are some new multicoverage products out there; for example, the traditional personal umbrella and business umbrella liability policies. *Umbrella policies* are designed so that an investor who owns an apartment building, a house, a duplex, and a piece of raw land can insure each one of those individually at the minimum amounts allowable, then purchase a blanket or an umbrella policy that stands in back of those policies. These are also called *excess coverage policies.* Sometimes these are more economical than large policies for each property, because the likelihood of having a liability-generating event on two or three separate properties at the same time is a lot less likely than having one at an individual property. The umbrella or excess coverage policies are generally reasonably priced and are usually worth consideration.

Other new policies are being offered. One of those is a *lawsuit protection policy.* Supposedly, this policy provides insurance coverage for the costs of defending a suit not otherwise covered by traditional insurance. In essence, it strictly covers the cost of hiring a lawyer and having a lawyer defend you against some type of claim that flows from one of your properties and is otherwise not covered under your traditional policy.

Many people try to cut expenses and carry only minimum insurance. With jury verdicts rising every year, however, adequate insurance is critical. But what happens when a lawsuit goes beyond the policy limit? Here are a few examples where that happened:

Jury Award: $995,000
A child fell to her death from an apartment window that was too close to the floor and lacked safety guards. (California, August 2004)

Jury Award: $1,500,000
A tenant sustained severe brain injury when she fell while descending a darkened flight of stairs at her apartment building. (California, July 2005)

Jury Award: $10,125,000
A 24-year-old tenant was seriously injured when he fell through a skylight on the roof of his apartment building. (California, April 2005)

Jury Award: $6,000,000
A boy burned his hands on the open flame of a gas stove. He was warming his hands because the apartment's heater did not work. (California, July 2007)

The examples above are all from California cases, but these types of lawsuits and jury verdicts occur in every state in the nation.

Setting Up Defense Barriers

Once you have set up your first line of defense (insurance), you have to think about those situations that go beyond the scope of your coverage. Remember, insurance is only your first barrier, and there are limits to your policy. If an incident causes damages that go beyond what your insurance will cover, the attorneys will go after the next deep pocket—that's you. Let's go back to our dog bite example. In this scenario, you own the duplex where the event occurred, and you are insured for $100,000/$300,000 insurance coverage. The child unfortunately is badly injured, spends weeks in the hospital, and has to have reconstructive surgery. In the end, the damages are between $400,000 and $500,000, and for argument's sake, let's say this seems like a valid lawsuit against you. What now? The flow of liability has come to your doorstep. It has gone from the tenant, who had very little assets, to the insurance company, which in this situation may have offered up the one-person policy limit of $100,000. (Insurance companies do not just offer up the policy limit without pretty good cause; however, at some point, when it becomes obvious that your legal defense will go beyond the scope of the policy, they are likely to pay the policy limit and then consider themselves off the hook.)

Now the lawyers are looking to you for the $300,000 to $400,000 in damages that have not been paid. What do you do about this amount for which you are now personally liable? You, being the asset protection–minded person you are, will have set up defensive barriers so that once the liability flows past the amount of the insurance, you are still able to stop the flow of liability from placing your other assets at risk. Obviously, if you have $1 million in equity in the duplex where the dog bite occurred, there is no stopping the attorneys from going after the equity of that property. No matter what kind of barriers you have set up, they will go after the equity in the duplex, because the location of the incident is the source of the liability and it has sufficient equity to pay for that liability. There is no escaping it. Really, what you are trying to defend is not the equity in the duplex but, rather, the equity in other properties, such as the equity in your residence or other personal assets.

How do you cap the liability flow once it has poured over the bounds of the insurance policy? This is where traditional entities, such as corporations, limited liability companies (LLCs), and irrevocable trusts, come into play. Figure 2.2 illustrates how the flow of liability generated by your investment can be stopped at the barrier which, in this case, is an LLC. The arrows leaving those investments can affect only the investments within their LLC and nothing outside of it.

Remember, your first line of defense should always be your insurance; your second line of defense is barriers that disrupt the flow of liability. As mentioned, some of those barriers include entities such as corporations, LLCs, and irrevocable trusts, which we are going to explore thoroughly in the chapters that follow. First let's take a look at the concept of *inside liability* and *outside liability*.

FIGURE 2.2 *Liability Flowing from an Investment Can Be Blocked by the Entity Barrier*

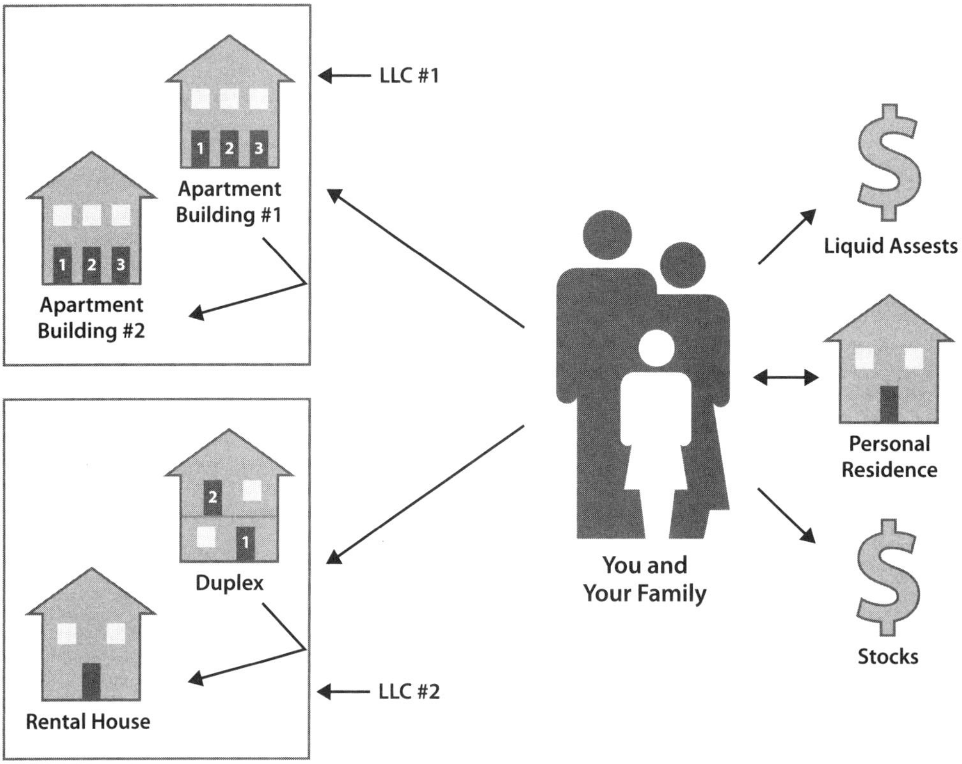

Inside and Outside Liability

One of the goals of asset protection planning is to place barriers to block or disrupt the flow of liability. The primary way to do so is to create a separate entity to hold investment property. If an entity is properly formed and the investment property is properly held by the entity, a liability barrier has been created. For assets contained in a separate entity, the liability flow question becomes one of inside liability and outside liability.

For example, let's say that Alice, Bill, and Charlie own an apartment building in a properly formed limited liability company named Main

Street Apartments LLC. In this example, the term *inside liability* refers to that liability (lawsuits) that arise from the ownership or operating of the apartment building. The general rule is that individual owners (members) of a limited liability company are not personally responsible for claims or judgments against the company. So in a situation where a tenant files a lawsuit, only the assets of the LLC would be at risk to those claims. In other words, Alice, Bill, and Charlie would not have to worry about the loss of their homes or other assets. Can they lose the apartment building? Yes. If the lawsuit was costly enough, all the assets of the Main Street Apartments LLC would be at risk. So in this case, inside liabilities are limited to the assets inside the LLC. If you look again at Figure 2.2, inside liability concerns the things contained *within* the individual LLC barriers.

The other consideration here is outside liability. The term *outside liability* refers to the liabilities of Alice, Bill, and Charlie individually and how they affect ownership of the assets within the LLC. Again, looking at Figure 2.2, outside liability concerns everything *outside* the LLC barriers. Here's an example:

> Let's say that Bill, as a sole proprietor, owned and operated a construction business that recently failed. One of the creditors of Bill's business filed a lawsuit against him and got a judgment for $1 million. That judgment, as it relates to the Main Street Apartments LLC, would be considered an outside liability. So the question becomes: Can Bill's judgment creditor seize the apartment building and sell it to satisfy the debt owed by Bill? No. The apartment building held inside the LLC is protected from potential claims against any individual member. The judgment creditor can't seize the assets of the LLC; instead, the creditor is limited to a remedy called a *charging order*. A creditor with a charging order against the member of the LLC is only permitted the right to whatever actual cash distributions are made by the LLC to the

debtor/member. The creditor can't force a distribution or seize any portion of the assets of the LLC.

We will take a much closer look at inside and outside liability protections for corporations, LLCs, and limited partnerships in the chapters focusing on those entity types.

The "Keep It Simple" Approach

Up to this point, we have talked about liability flow basics, and we have learned that liability can flow to or from an individual. Likewise, the more properties, businesses, and ventures an individual has, the more likely that a liability or lawsuit will threaten all of the assets collectively. We also learned that the first line of defense in asset protection is always to purchase and maintain an appropriate amount of insurance. From there, we saw how creating entities to hold assets or businesses can stop the flow of liability or help protect the assets from outside liabilities.

At this point, you may be thinking that it would be best just to have a separate corporation, LLC, or irrevocable trust for every individual property you have. By doing this, each individual asset would be protected from all the others. This might be a good idea, but the problems with this approach are (a) the cost involved, (b) the complexity of setting it up, and (c) the ongoing administration of it. I've been to seminars and read books about some pretty extensive and sometimes mind-boggling asset protection plans. Lots of estate-planning gurus subscribe to the idea that the more entities created or the more complicated an asset protection plan is, the better it will protect. Sometimes these proposed plans seem so convoluted, I find myself wondering who would need this kind of asset protection planning. I don't necessarily subscribe to the "more is better" philosophy, and most of my clients share my preference for keeping it straightforward. Make it reasonably effective, but keep it simple.

Grouping Properties

Balance is necessary. Most people like the idea of having some basic asset protection, but you have to weigh that against the costs involved and the additional layers of administrative complexity. How you balance those needs is based on your own personal level of discomfort or paranoia, just as with choosing how much insurance to purchase. Investor's face a certain amount of anxiety, and the ultimate goal is to reduce it to a minimum while realizing that eliminating it is pretty much impossible. However, some people do go over the top trying to eliminate risk. Let me give you an example:

> Imagine you have ten properties and you are quite concerned about the liability flow potentially affecting all of those properties. To maximize your protection, you create a separate entity for each property. Each of those ten entities will require various annual formalities, such as shareholder meetings and other annual meetings. Your state government may require each entity to pay an annual fee, say $800, and each entity will have separate state and federal tax returns. Just these tasks alone will become quite cumbersome, and the investor will likely be so busy maintaining these entities that she will grow tired of the effort.

As an investor, you need to achieve a balance between feeling comfortable with your asset protection and keeping your sanity.

What is the right mix? As I said earlier, everybody has a different comfort level. Likewise, different properties have different risk characteristics. So, for example, somebody might own ten properties with three of those properties being very risky. For those three, the ideal situation might be to put each one of them in a separate LLC or other entity. But then you would have three more tax returns, three more yearly bills, three more sets of minutes, and three more attorney's fees. A smarter (and simpler) approach might be to identify the three properties with the highest potential liability and put them all into one LLC. Returning to the ten-property example above, that leaves us with seven more to deal with. These less risky properties might be combined into a second LLC or entity. The goal would be to keep those two entities separate from each other and separate from the personal assets of the investor.

By *personal assets,* I am referring to things like a primary home, a second home, bank accounts, financial investments, etc. Generally speaking, personal assets like a primary residence would never go into an asset protection entity, because they are very low liability generators and significant tax advantages, like the primary home tax exemption, would be lost.

For most people, the simple approach is advisable. The trick is to look across the board at what you own and try to figure out how many separate entities you really need. Then ask yourself, "Is this number of entities intelligent, or am I getting unnecessarily overcomplicated?" Using a simple approach means assessing which properties have similar levels of liability risk and grouping them together. When looking at a low-risk property, one might even consider keeping it out of an entity altogether. This is advisable if the property has a liability risk so low that you feel very little stress about that asset.

To further illustrate, let's return to our example of ten properties:

> We still have the three big apartment buildings that are high liability. In addition to this, let's say we have three duplexes, two triplexes, and a fourplex. There is some concern about liability on these six properties but nothing significant. And let's say that the tenth property is a house that you rent to a family member. The family member has been there for eight years and doesn't want to move, and you don't want to sell the house. That house presumably has a very low risk of generating liability. You may not want or need to put that house in some type of entity with other properties, because the other, higher-risk properties may pose a

threat to the equity you have in that house. So, here we might have one LLC with the three apartment buildings, another LLC with six income properties, and the rental house remaining in the investor's personal name.

This is a simple example of differentiating your liability risk for different properties. In a case where a client owns ten rental houses, each individually might be viewed as a low-risk property, but as a group, the risk goes up significantly. In that case, two asset protection entities containing five houses each might be a good approach. There's no set rule on how to group properties; the grouping should be done in a way that makes you comfortable.

Separating Equity

Once you have made an initial assessment of how many entities you need based upon liability-generating risk, do you need to assess anything else? Yes. Another very important factor when assessing how to group properties into entities is how much equity each property has. Let's return to the previous ten-property example:

> We have the three apartment buildings that represented the highest likelihood of generating liability. Let's say they are all 24-unit apartment buildings. They are all in the same kind of neighborhood, and all have a similar risk level. So far, it looks like these three properties should go in the same entity. Now let's look at the equity situation. Let's say each one of these apartment buildings is worth $2 million. We will call these three buildings A, B, and C.
>
> - Building A is worth $2 million, you have owned it for five years, and real estate values have been consistent for that time. You put 30 percent down and have a 70 percent loan-to-value

ratio on that building; therefore, there is 30 percent equity, or $600,000 of equity in an ideal world.
- Property B is similar in all respects: same aging, same kind of loan, same equity considerations. You, therefore, have two properties that are pretty similar. Between these two buildings, you have an estimated $1.2 million in equity.
- Building C, however, is different. Building C is something you inherited or bought many years ago, and the mortgage on that building is only about $300,000. It's still similar in almost all other respects to Buildings A and B, but Building C has $1.7 million in equity.

Should Building C still go in the same entity with Buildings A and B? The answer is almost certainly no. You don't want to group it with A or B; instead, you would probably want a separate entity for C. Why expose all that extra equity to the potential creditors of Buildings A and B? So, even though these three properties are similar in other respects, one represents more of your wealth and should be given a more protected, separate existence. By being sectioned off, it might be at risk from its own inside liabilities but not from the debts or liabilities of Buildings A or B.

Shifting Equity and Equity Stripping

The above example of separating high-equity properties from high-liability properties was essential for illustrating that equity is an important factor when deciding how to determine which assets should go together in an entity. But in some circumstances, a better approach might be to keep the high-risk properties together and shift equity to other, low-liability risk properties. Staying with our ten-property example above, let's say we have three entities:

Entity 1 contains the two high-risk, low-equity Buildings A and B. Entity 2 contains the high-risk, high-equity Building C. Let's say that the third entity, Entity 3, has the six moderately low-risk properties. And remember the house is on its own; it is not in an entity at all because it is very low risk.

Now let's consider that one of the properties in Entity 3, a fourplex, is a low-liability property in a good part of town and you plan on keeping it forever. However, you have a large mortgage on that particular property. Assume for this example that the financing interest rates are all the same, meaning that no matter which of your properties you are borrowing on, the rate is the same. (I know that's not how it works in the real world, but for the sake of illustration, let's assume it is.) What you have now is a high-risk property with a lot of equity (Building C) and a low-risk property with very little equity (the fourplex). You would be wise to *shift* some of your equity from Building C to the fourplex. By placing a higher mortgage on Building C and using the excess funds to pay down the mortgage on the fourplex, you have effectively shifted your equity from a higher-risk property to a lower-risk property. Shifting equity like this lets you arrange your assets and entities in such a way that your relatively low-risk, and separately protected, properties represent the majority of your real estate equity.

Shifting equities like this allows you to group your properties more intelligently. Shifting the equity as we did in the above example means that Building C can now be grouped with Buildings A and B, meaning you now may only need two entities, Entity 1 containing Buildings A, B, and C and Entity 2 containing the six low-risk properties. Going back to the reason we are creating these entities in the first place, if a lawsuit occurs because of an event in the Building C entity, the equity you moved is safely located somewhere else. You will have successfully protected more of your assets.

In summary, understanding liability flow and inside liabilities and outside liabilities helps you to understand the need for using entities in asset protection planning. Grouping your properties by risk level, separating high-equity properties, and shifting equity to lower-risk properties are all ways to help you cluster your investments into meaningful, similar groups. Most importantly, proper planning can reduce the total number of entities needed and the costs involved, making asset protection effective while still keeping it simple.

3 Forces That Affect Your Entity Choice

WHEN YOU DECIDE to use some type of entity structure, different factors influence which entity type is the best. Many times, people choose one entity only to wish later they had chosen another. Perhaps they were focused on keeping the start-up costs low but find out the ongoing costs are higher than necessary. Maybe privacy and security were initial goals, but by accomplishing those, they got blindsided by higher taxes. You really can't make an informed choice unless you examine all possible factors and find some equilibrium that balances the different aspects of each entity. When you have found that equilibrium and all of the factors balance out in a way that is amenable to you, then you've likely found your proper entity, whether it's an LLC, a trust, a corporation, or some other type. There is no single best choice. You're going to have to find the balance that's best in your situation.

Looking at Figure 3.1, you will see that some considerations include taxes, state laws, personal business needs, asset protection features, yearly costs, and degree of complexity. At the top of the list of forces that affect the choice of entity are taxes. Taxes undoubtedly influence more decisions

FIGURE 3.1 *Forces That Pull at Your Entity Choice*

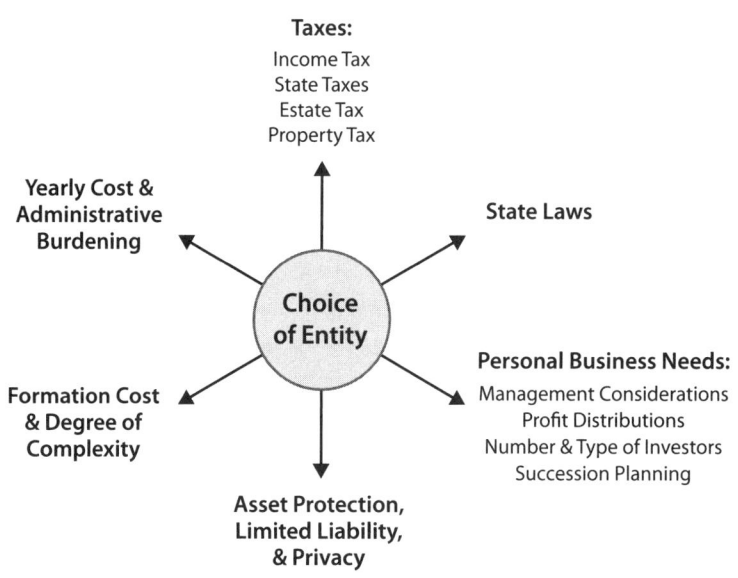

in this area than any other factor. We'll take an in-depth look at tax considerations in the next chapter; for now, let's take a closer look at the other items on the list.

State Laws

Some state laws dictate the type of entity that can be used for specific types of ventures, projects, or actions being performed within the entity. Likewise, not all states allow all the different entity types. For example, only a handful of states allow the formation of a limited liability limited partnership or series limited liability company (LLC), so generally you'd want to rule those out right away. It is possible to form one of those entity types in, say, Delaware, and operate it in another state, but if you can accomplish the same goals in a less-complicated way, that approach is preferable. This makes looking at the laws in your state a great starting point, because you might find some concrete reasons why you should or should not choose a particular entity type for your real estate investment. In the Appendix, I have included a list of websites for each state's laws.

Personal Business Needs

Another category of factors that influence entity choice is personal business needs. Generally, people come in with taxes, asset protection, and some personal needs in mind when they start the process of forming their entities. Personal needs comprise a fairly substantial category, because there are certain things people want to accomplish with their entities. Personal needs are a big portion of the conversation that I have with clients as I'm discussing the various entities and what might be appropriate for them. Some of the considerations we need to look at include management issues, profit distributions, type of investors, and succession planning.

Management Issues

Who will manage the entity and what the management roles will be are important considerations. When the client has the management roles well defined, sometimes the discussion is very straightforward, and a particular entity emerges quickly as the best choice. Even with management roles defined, however, sometimes other factors come into play, and one entity type does not stand out.

Profit Distributions

How a client wants the profits of an entity to be distributed is also important. Profit distributions for a subchapter S corporation are completely different from the variable profit distribution plan that can be employed with an LLC. Likewise, general partnerships may have one distribution requirement, while a limited partnership may have a completely different one.

Number and Type of Investors

The number and type of investors that might be in an entity are also important. For my average client, there will be one or two (generally not more than five) investors. Usually, the situation is relatively simple, such as a couple of brothers who want to buy a building. Occasionally, though, I have eight to ten people come in who want to form a corporation for the purpose of a joint venture (e.g., a subdivision, an apartment building conversion to condos, etc.). The first thing these eight to ten people need to consider is how many investors there will be and if there will be any future investors. Will stock be sold, or will other investors be brought on board in exchange for stock or membership interests? If the answer is yes, the entity choice becomes much more complicated and needs to be discussed with an attorney.

Succession Planning

Another personal business need that may affect your entity choice is whether you are thinking ahead to succession planning. Some people generically refer to this in the broader category of "estate planning." But actually, there are two distinct subsets of estate planning: tax planning and succession planning. Some people don't have an estate tax problem per se, but they still need to think about how assets will eventually pass to their children or heirs. In the next chapter, we will look at estate tax planning, but here we are focusing on moving assets from one generation to the next.

With succession planning in mind, many of my clients choose to get their children involved in the management and operation of their real estate investments. Certain types of entities are better at facilitating that process. For example, succession planning might dictate the choice of entity for parents who own four or five large-scale apartment buildings and want to hand those assets down to the next generation. The parents may need to decide whether the assets go to their children in their own names or as a form of stock or an LLC interest. The choice may impact whether the client's children can quickly take over management of the properties in case of an emergency or when the parents pass away. All of these factors are important if succession planning is part of a client's needs in deciding what entity to use.

Succession planning provides a good example of how equilibrium between factors can be established. If succession planning is a very important component of your entity choice, then perhaps you would consider a family limited partnership. Family limited partnerships can be fairly complicated and administratively burdensome; however, the ease of succession and possible estate tax benefits could balance out this burden.

Asset Protection, Limiting Liability, and Privacy

The next considerations are asset protection, limiting liability, and privacy concerns. Let's start with asset protection and limiting liability. Although they sound the same, when people talk about *asset protection*, they are referring to the methods available to protect assets from liabilities arising elsewhere. *Limiting liability* conversations are usually exactly the opposite, concerning the ability to stop or constrain liability to the asset or activity from which it arises. These two ideas are closely related but nonetheless separate considerations. In situations where you have more than one source of assets, you are likely trying to achieve both goals. Knowing whether your goal is to have asset protection, limited liability, or both will help dictate what style of entity to use.

Privacy is also an important factor for many of my clients. One of those asset protection "pearls of wisdom" you often hear is that if you don't own anything, you won't get sued. According to this line of thinking, one of the best ways to avoid lawsuits is to appear to be broke. If you subscribe to this line of thinking and your goal is that your name never appear as the owner of any property, then certain types of entities are better suited for this purpose.

This desire for privacy has been a springboard for many asset protection seminars. Many seminar marketers propose the use of different states in establishing your entities. Until recently, Nevada had a reputation for keeping the owners of an entity private. Those rules have changed, however, and the rules nationwide are constantly in flux. So what you thought was going to allow you a degree of privacy last year may do nothing of the kind a few years down the road. In addition to touting out-of-state entity formations, the promoters of seminars often propose the use of private trustees as the named manager or officer of your entity. The logic is that if someone looked up the owner of the property, all they would see is the name of some entity. Then further inquiry as to who owned the entity would only show the name of some out-of-state trustee. Since the proposed trustee is private, there would be no easy way to get any additional information.

Some find these kinds of plans appealing. Unfortunately, they're also very expensive and problematic. First, the cost of assembling this multilayered, multientity asset protection plan is usually pretty steep. In addition, the ongoing administrative costs and trustee fees are frequently fairly expensive. Add to that the fact that these types of asset protection plans can cause serious problems with insuring and refinancing properties. Likewise, moving properties around to accomplish these fairly complicated plans sometimes results in a property's being reassessed for property tax purposes. Keep in mind, if you're trying to make it appear that you don't own the property anymore, the county tax assessor's office will likely see your actions as a transfer of ownership and take that opportunity to reassess property taxes. In asset protection planning, it is always safe to assume that the more privacy you want, the more complicated your asset protection plan will be. I have always found asset protection plans that rely too heavily on privacy to be very problematic and have never been able to recommend one to a client.

Don't get me wrong: I agree that privacy is an important component of asset protection, but it should not be the primary goal. In the previous chapter, we talked about insurance being the first line of defense and asset protection entities being second. Privacy considerations should take a backseat to both of them. Privacy will never really help you if somebody gets a judgment against you and is intent on collecting on it. Why? Because there's a procedure in civil courts called a *debtor's hearing*. When a judgment holder thinks you are hiding assets, they have the right to have the court subpoena you for an appearance. In that appearance, you will be placed under oath asked questions about all of your financial dealings and all of your assets. You will be standing in a courtroom, and you will have to answer all of the questions put to you under penalty of perjury. At that point, most people give up their assets rather than take a chance on going to jail.

Does that mean you should give up on trying to keep your assets private? Absolutely not—it just shouldn't be your primary goal. You may not be able to keep your assets private all the time, but making a reasonable effort to keep them private some of the time is definitely worthwhile. To put it another way:

> You can hide all of your assets some of the time, and you can hide some of your assets all of the time, but you can never hide all of your assets all of the time.

For example, if you use some common sense, you can make it difficult for the general public to see what you own, and that can come in very handy in an initial asset assessment by a plaintiff or lawyer who is considering a lawsuit. Remember, when attorneys are determining whether to go after you, they are usually first looking to your insurance and then to your other assets, but not always. If a lawsuit is going to allege causes of action that are generally not covered by insurance (e.g., sexual or racial discrimination), the lawyers want to know, up front, that you have enough assets to make a lawsuit worthwhile. If they can't see any property or other asset ownership through the county and state records, they may be discouraged from filing the lawsuit. In some cases, you can prevent a lawsuit by simply presenting yourself as a poor target—as not having deep pockets.

Formation Costs and Degree of Complexity

Some entity types are inherently more expensive. The level of complexity goes from the simple and straightforward to the mind-bogglingly complex. The sole proprietorship is the simplest of all the entities, and if you form it in your own name, the formalities will be very few. From there, the next level of complexity is the sole proprietorship done with a fictitious name; this is also called a *doing business as* (DBA), and a little formality is involved but not much. Unfortunately, with that simplicity comes the absolute risk of personal liability.

Next are the general partnerships, which are more complex because more than one person is involved; thus, there is more than one set of ideas, profit distributions, investment ratios, etc. to be reconciled. The general partnership can be as simple as two people buying a property together without any formal agreement. Once again, general partnerships can be simple, but each of the partners has personal liability exposure. Worse, each partner is individually liable for 100 percent of the partnership. This is called being *jointly and severally liable*.

From the general partnership, we move up to the limited partnership, of which the basic foundation must be a *partnership agreement*. This is because the very nature of a limited partnership differentiates between a general partner and a limited partner. The purpose, of course, is to limit the liability and, thus, the involvement and management of at least one of the partners. A limited partnership requires a more sophisticated agreement, so there's more effort and/or expense involved, but the reward is that at least one of the partners will have limited liability.

From there, we move up to the entities that require a more regimented formation. These include the subchapter S corporations,

C corporations, and LLCs. Corporations and LLCs come into creation via documents that need to be filed with the state. Corporations, whether C or S corporations, require the filing of articles of incorporation. If the corporation is an S corporation, a designation must be made to show the IRS that the entity is electing to do business as an S corporation. Additionally, a form must be filed with the state taxation entity in the state of incorporation that shows that the entity is choosing a subchapter S corporation style. LLCs require the filing of the articles of organization. Articles of organization can sometimes look a lot like articles of incorporation. However, an LLC is not being incorporated; it is being organized. Thus, it files articles of organization rather than articles of incorporation. The differences are important. Likewise, these entities require internal documentations. The bylaws, minutes, and resolutions of a corporation must be drafted and formalized by the corporation to be valid. There are similar internal documents for LLCs as well. In drafting these documents, the complexity generally goes beyond what the average person can handle.

Many people have an idea of what type of entity they want to use. Perhaps they got some advice from one of their friends or did some reading on the Internet; maybe they even went to a seminar and now feel ready to get started. But after they start looking at what's necessary, they begin to realize that their preconceived notion of what they wanted will be more complex and expensive than expected. For example, I had a client come to me with a rather elaborate plan in mind involving having a corporation act as the managing member of an LLC. The LLC membership interests would be owned by four separate property trusts (one for each of his adult children). Structures like this can be implemented and may fit exactly what the client needs in a specific situation, but for most property investors, this type of plan has a level of complexity (and expense) that's unnecessary. Likewise, many of the client's objectives can almost always be met in other, less complicated ways. That being the case, you don't want to run into problems with your entity because of a level of complexity that makes it difficult for you (and maybe your accountant) to understand. If you can't clearly understand the workings of the asset protection plan, the chance of making a mistake is much more likely.

By the same token, the more complex something gets, the more expensive it gets. If you have entities holding entities that distribute out to spendthrift/separate property trusts, your formation costs will be very high. Each one of those parts costs money to create, and sometimes the attorney's fees for this type of work are hard to swallow. Simple approaches usually work for most businesses and real estate investors, so it is usually best to start with these. Needless to say, choosing your entity will be dictated, in part, by the level of complexity and the cost of formation with which you are comfortable.

Yearly Cost and Administrative Burden

The next factors that affect your choice of entity are ongoing yearly costs and administrative burdens. Just like formation costs and degree of complexity, yearly administrative burdens and annual costs sometimes exceed a client's comfort level. Each entity should be considered in relation to its ongoing annual cost. In addition, multiple entities can get very expensive. Many of the attorneys in real estate asset protection advocate the use of a separate LLC for each property. This approach seems pretty straightforward and easy to understand, but if a person owns a lot of properties, there would be a lot of LLCs to contend with. If they are located or doing business in a state like California, then each of the LLCs would have its own annual fees, becoming very costly year after year. It might be smarter to group properties intelligently and have fewer LLCs.

Another problem with having too many entities is the tax filing requirements. Having many different entities means you may have to file many different tax returns each year. Perhaps you are thinking that all you have to do is write a check to your accountant and he will deal with that burden for you. However, the taxes will still be costly. There is no getting around the fact that having many entities is cumbersome and expensive, so only create the entities you really need and only when you really need them.

Getting the Right Advice

The main problem with people seeking out professionals is cost. Something in the back of most investors' minds tells them that they need to get the right advice. Mistakes are very costly, and a lot of bad advice flies around out there. Most of the free advice is so convoluted that even if you found the right type of advice, you would not know it when you saw it. Likely, four or five other competing advisors would offer different opinions; how are you supposed to sift through all that?

It is amazing how often a client has read something on the Internet, bought some tapes, or gone to some seminar and now has a skewed view of how things work. And as the client is telling me what she is trying to accomplish, I'm amazed at how incorrect the information is. On top of this proliferation of misinformation, there are also "formation services" that will form entities for you. These are the typical online incorporation document filing services that claim to do it all for some low fee, but those sales pitches are not even close to reality. All you have to do is read the disclaimer to realize that you are probably going to have problems—and that you'll be on your own when you do. Of course, all anyone actually gets from these companies is a piece of paper that is stamped by the Department of Corporations (or whatever entity formation department your particular state has). They don't care if that entity is actually the correct one for you; they put the burden on you to get appropriate legal advice and know which entity is best. Also, they use their one-size-fits-all logic for everybody. If asset protection were really that simple, why would you be reading this book?

Sometimes the people who use online services create serious problems for themselves by trying to take shortcuts. One of the most common is transferring property into their newly formed entity and triggering a reassessment of taxes; the online people didn't tell them about the potential tax consequences of transferring property. That's just one of many mistakes that, unfortunately, people who use online services will not know about until it's too late.

My advice is that you always consult an attorney and an accountant. I am aware that attorneys' fees and accountants' fees may seem expensive, but a mistake in this area can be a lot more costly. For example, in the state of California, when you transfer a property into an entity, the owners of that entity must notify the county tax assessor's office and provide the proper documentation to avoid a reassessment of taxes. A common mistake is to file these documents improperly or forget to file them at all, and sometimes the mistake is devastating. Maybe the original taxes were based on an historical value of, say, $100,000 for a property that now currently has a $1 million market value. When that property is reassessed, the annual property tax increases from approximately $1,250 per year based on $100,000 assessed value to $12,500 a year based on the reassessed value of $1 million. This is usually the point where the investor finally decides that seeing an attorney or an accountant is necessary. Unfortunately, a mistake that triggers a reassessment of property taxes is very difficult to undo. You can't just say, "Never mind. I didn't really mean to do that."

The fact that you are considering using an LLC, a corporation, or some other entity shows that you know your business dealings require a level of forethought. Mistakes can be expensive and defeat everything you're trying to accomplish. Avoid the online incorporation scams, the traveling seminars, and the "corporations in a box." If you are interested in protecting your assets, getting the appropriate legal and accounting advice is the only intelligent approach, so why not do it right?

4 Choosing the Entity Type: Tax Considerations

TAX CONSIDERATIONS ARE always, *always* a huge part of choosing an entity type. It is great to protect your assets, but if you end up paying twice the taxes, the protection strategy may not be worth it. It is great to be able to bubble off or separate out entities and ventures so that they do not adversely affect each other, but if in doing that, you trigger taxation that could have been avoided, you won't be happy.

In the previous chapter, we looked at the other forces that impact the entity choice. Now we will focus on the four types of taxes that concern your assets.

Just as it is essential to discuss the appropriateness and complexity of choosing an entity with your attorney, it is crucial that you understand the possible tax ramifications as well. Usually, this means you need to have a conversation with your accountant. Here, however, I want to offer a word of caution. When you go to your accountant, you need to explain that you are not solely interested in creating an entity for tax purposes; make sure your accountant understands that your primary goal is asset protection. If your accountant doesn't understand your asset protection motivation, he is likely to give you an answer based only on whether employing the use of an entity is good from a tax perspective. I have had quite a few clients say, "My accountant told me that I don't really need an LLC or a corporation because it really won't help me taxwise." It may be true that neither of those entities would improve their tax situations, but what happened to the primary goal of asset protection and limiting liability? If you don't let your accountant know what you're trying to accomplish, her answers might lead you in the wrong direction. Remember, asset protection is not normally in an accountant's realm of education or expertise. Conversely, your attorney is probably not as savvy about taxes. Therefore, it's probably a good idea to plan on getting both involved.

As you saw from Figure 3.1, four types of taxes need consideration: income taxes, state taxes, property taxes, and estate taxes.

Income Taxes: Double-Taxed or Pass-Through Entity?

The method of taxation for an entity is always a primary consideration. You might devise the best asset protection plan in the world, but no one would use it if taxes doubled as a result. What does *pass-through entity* mean? It means that certain entities "pass through" all income and profits to the owners, shareholders, or beneficiaries, and the return on investment is taxed at that level.

On the other hand, C corporations and certain trusts are examples of entities that pay taxes at the corporate or trust (entity) level and then again at the individual shareholder or beneficiary level. This structure is commonly referred to as *double taxed,* and in most cases when I use the term, it will refer to C corporations. Think of Microsoft, Apple, or any of the other big corporations when you are picturing a separately taxed entity. These large corporations file an income tax return and pay taxes. Then with whatever is left (the net profit of the corporation), they make distributions to the shareholders. The shareholders then have to pay taxes on those distributions. So the profit that came into the corporation is taxed once at the corporate level and again at the individual shareholder level. Because of this double taxation, separately taxed entities are almost always to be avoided. The only reason you would want to have a separately taxed entity is if you have the structure of one of those big, publicly traded corporations. Hopefully, those structures also have efficient accounting departments whose job is to minimize the taxes at the corporate level.

In addition to C corporations, some of the more elaborate asset protection plans include sophisticated trusts, which are sometimes double taxed as well. Generally speaking, both C corporations and those specialized trusts provide a good measure of asset protection but are not well suited for real estate investments because of the double taxation.

The obvious choice for the average person who owns some real estate is a pass-through entity. But by choosing a pass-through entity, have you then eliminated the use of a corporation as your entity? No, because there is more than one type of corporation. We just ruled out C corporations, and nonprofit corporations don't have much use in asset protection planning. This leaves us with S corporations.

The *S* in S corporation does not stand for "small," as some people may think. It stands for subchapter S of the treasury codes. The subchapter S regulations provide that, if a timely election is made, a corporation may be taxed as a pass-through entity. Hence, the name of these entities became "S corporation." As mentioned above, you have to elect to be a subchapter S corporation. When you form a corporation, the presumption is that you are a C corporation unless you say otherwise. An election (IRS Form 2553) must be filed to tell the IRS that, as a corporate body, the corporation elects to have income and profits passed directly through to the shareholders. The process of filing this form is fairly straightforward, but the formality must be completed.

Other than C corporations and those specialized trusts, just about every entity choice worth considering is a pass-through entity of some type. Partnerships, limited partnerships, family limited partnerships, and limited liability companies all share the S corporation's pass-through tax characteristics. Of these options, S corporations have the most rigid formal structure. Because the structure is so formal and so many other pass-through entities are available, some suggest that the S corporation is no longer a preferred entity for real estate investments. That may be true for the most part, but in some situations, the S corporation is still the perfect fit. That brings us to our next income tax consideration: dealer property versus investor property.

Dealer Property versus Investor Property

One truly ambiguous tax topic in real estate investment is the dealer versus investor distinction. The amount of income tax you pay and the tax advantages available to you in a real estate investment may change drastically depending on whether the IRS labels you an investor or a dealer. Investor versus dealer status is one of those areas of real estate tax law that can truly drive you nuts trying to figure it out. If you sell multiple properties in any single tax year or a few properties over the course of two or three years, you may find yourself at risk of being labeled a dealer.

Unfortunately, there is no real distinction, test, or recognized "number of properties sold" criterion that determines whether a person has crossed a line into dealer status. You may come across real estate agents or accountants who will tell you that if you sell fewer than three or five properties per year, then you will not be considered a dealer. Unfortunately, this street wisdom isn't based on fact. Nothing in the tax code or in case law sets any definitive number of properties as a dividing line between dealer and investor status. This ambiguity, compounded with possible severe tax consequences, has caused more than a few sleepless nights for real estate investors. With this in mind, this section will try to shed some light on dealer versus investor status issues and offer some ways to avoid potential problems.

Who Is a Property Dealer?

A *real estate dealer* is a person who is involved on a regular basis in the development, improvement, and advertisement of property for sale. Subdividers and developers are almost always labeled dealers. However, even if you are not a subdivider or developer, you may be labeled a dealer if your real estate activities rise to the level of a trade or business in which your property investments appear more like inventory to be sold than long-term investments.

Who Is a Property Investor?

Unlike a dealer, a *property investor* is a person who generally holds real estate for appreciation and/or cash flow from rental activities. Doesn't everyone invest in real estate with the hope that it will appreciate? Yes, but the IRS says there are two categories of real estate investment. For the sake of clarity, let's call them *buy-to-sell (dealer) properties* and *buy-to-hold (investor) properties*.

Why Does It Matter If You Are a Dealer or an Investor?

Our tax rules favor the investor over the dealer. An investor holding property in his own name files a Schedule E for investment properties and a Schedule D for reporting profits from the sale of an investment property. Schedule D profits qualify for capital gains tax rates—15 percent for federal taxes in 2008—and are not considered income from employment. A dealer holding property in her own name, however, is forced to report operations and profits from the sale of her buy-to-sell real estate on a Schedule C as ordinary income and expenses. That's a bad thing because, generally speaking, ordinary income tax rates are higher than capital gains tax rates. Let's take a look at an example:

> Let's say two people, Carl and Clint, buy two similar investment/rental properties. Both are single-family homes, and both have a purchase price of $300,000. Now let's say that both Carl

and Clint make $20,000 in improvements to their properties and the market value of each of the properties grows to $420,000 in 18 months (hot market). At that time, both properties are sold. Let's assume both Carl and Clint collected rent and depreciated their respective properties on their tax returns. Let's further assume this is Carl's first investment property but Clint has bought and sold four or five other similar houses in the last few years.

In the example above, the tax situation for Carl looks fairly straightforward. He has made the investment a capital asset by keeping it for more than 12 months, and his intention was to buy to hold. He will have some amount of recapture of depreciation tax to deal with, but the gain on the property will be federally taxed at the long-term capital gains rate (currently 15 percent). As such, Carl's federal taxes on the gain will be approximately ($120,000 appreciation − $20,000 improvements) × 0.15 = $15,000.

Clint, on the other hand, may have very different results. If the IRS decides to label Clint a real estate dealer, a couple of things happen. First, any depreciation Clint has taken on the property will be disallowed. Second, all of the profit on the sale of the property will be taxed at federal ordinary income rates (as high as 35 percent in 2008). Third, the profit from the sale, now relabeled ordinary income, will trigger self-employment taxes that can be as high as 14.5 percent. As such, Clint would owe as much as $39,000 on the gain plus any self-employment taxes.

Obviously, there's a huge difference between Carl's and Clint's tax consequences. To make matters even worse, we really need to expand the example to consider how these things can quickly get out of control. In the real world, investors usually try to avoid paying taxes on the sale of real estate. One common way to do that is called a *1031 exchange*. Under the rules of a 1031 exchange, an investor is allowed to sell one real estate investment and replace it with another without triggering capital gains tax. Here's an example:

Using the same facts as above, let's assume both Carl and Clint decided not to cash out their investments but instead did 1031 exchanges into other properties. Moreover, let's say that Clint has been doing exchanges all along, selling one fixed-up property and exchanging into the next fixer-upper.

In Carl's case there's no problem. As a property *investor*, Carl can do a tax-deferred exchange into another property as long as he conforms to ordinary 1031 exchange requirements.

Clint, on the other hand, has a big problem. If the IRS labels Clint a property *dealer*, things can get really ugly. Keep in mind that Clint won't be reporting his most recent exchange until it is completed and he is doing his taxes for that calendar year. Also, keep in mind that IRS audits don't happen instantly. It might be a year or two after he files his taxes before the IRS gets around to auditing Clint. If the audit results in Clint being labeled a real estate dealer, the IRS will disallow his exchange, triggering immediate income taxes, self-employment taxes, plus interest and possible penalties in cases of willful neglect or fraud.

To make matters worse, if Clint is labeled a dealer, the IRS will surely base its dealer determination partially on the number of properties Clint has sold in recent years. In our example, Clint had bought and sold four or five other similar houses over a few years and done exchanges with those as well. The IRS will likely disallow each of Clint's previous exchanges, triggering, in each case, more immediate taxes, interest, and any self-employment taxes not paid in those previous years.

Hopefully, you are starting to see the potentially dire consequences of being labeled a real estate dealer. We have already established that there are no set rules regarding how many properties you can sell before being labeled a dealer. So how long do you have to hold a property to be sure you won't be labeled a dealer when you sell it—one year, two, five? No one knows. None of those time periods is a barrier to being labeled a dealer. There are no rules.

With no set number of sales and no set holding period in the regulations, how does the IRS label a person a dealer? Everything hinges on your *intent* at the time you buy the property. If you purchased the property with the intent of holding it for income and appreciation benefits, then you are an investor. If, instead, you purchased the property with the intent of reselling it, then you are a dealer. Right now, you may be saying, "Wait a second. Everyone buys a property with the intent of eventually reselling it for a profit!" Yes, but nevertheless, this is the distinction the IRS and the courts use to differentiate between an investor and a dealer.

How does the IRS know what your intent was at the time you bought the property? How are the auditors going to climb into your head and know what you were thinking when you bought the property? They don't have to. In law, there is a concept called *burden of proof*. Usually, the burden of proof rests on the asserter, meaning that the person who makes an assertion has the responsibility of proving it. For example, if you are charged with a crime, it's the prosecutor's burden to prove it. If someone sues you, that person has the burden of proving you did something wrong. In both of these examples, if the person with the burden of proof fails to "prove it," the plantiff loses the case or lawsuit. With the IRS, however, the burden of proof is often shifted to the taxpayer. This means that all the IRS has to do is assert that your intent was to resell the property; then *you* have the burden of "proving" it's not true. If you fail to prove that you actually intended to hold the property for income and appreciation, you lose.

As you can imagine, this dealer versus investor issue leads to a lot of tax court litigation and appeals. What criteria do the courts use to determine if a person is a dealer or an investor? Unfortunately, the court decisions are almost as ambiguous as the IRS's definitions. Courts usually look to other court decisions to see how a determination has been made in the past. However, in one case, a court reviewing the other courts' decisions stated that the dealer versus investor issue was "engulfed in a fog of decisions with gossamer-like distinctions, and a quagmire of unworkable, unreliable, and often irrelevant tests" [*U.S. v. Winthrop, 417 F.2d 905, 906 (5th Cir. 1969).*] That colorful language pretty much sums it up. Over time, a list of criteria has emerged that the tax courts apply on a case-by-case basis. The courts have consistently held that no single factor is controlling in any given case and that each case must stand on its own set of circumstances. With that said, here are some of the factors the courts use in determining dealer status:

- *How long the property was held.* Properties held for less than two years appear more like dealer property.
- *The number of sales by the taxpayer in that year.* Although this is very important, there is no definitive number. Even one sale can make the property a dealer property if the intent was to resell rather than to invest.
- *The types of improvements made to the property.* The more extensive the improvements, the more likely the property was intended for resale.
- *The purpose of acquiring the property.*
- *The amount of income from the property sales compared to the taxpayer's other income.*
- *Extent and nature of efforts to sell the property.* Constant advertising and control agents are seen as characteristics of a dealer.
- *The subdivision and development of the property.*
- *The use of a business office to sell the property.*

You may think that some of these factors would be present whether a property was bought to sell or bought to hold. I agree. Nevertheless, these are the factors the tax court uses to determine if a person's actions add up to a pattern of regular, frequent, and continuous sales meriting a dealer designation.

Because the courts have stated that a determination must be made on a property-by-property basis, it's possible that a taxpayer can be considered a dealer with respect to some properties and an investor with respect to others. This is a very important concept, because many people with mostly buy-to-hold properties run across good fixer-uppers occasionally that they buy simply to fix up and sell. The danger is, if a person does too many of these buy-to-sell properties, then the IRS may decide to label that investor a dealer. If so labeled, you run a significant risk that the IRS will lump all of your buy-to-hold properties into the dealer category as well. You may be able to cleanse the taint from your buy-to-hold property by meeting the burden of proof on a property-by-property basis, but you definitely do not want to find yourself in this predicament. Remember, a real estate dealer is not entitled to depreciation, so if the IRS says you are a dealer, you may lose any depreciation write-offs you have taken, not just on your buy-to-sell properties but also on your buy-to-hold properties. Obviously, if the IRS disallows previously taken depreciation, you will probably face back taxes and interest.

Possible Ways to Avoid Being Labeled a Dealer

So how does all this dealer versus investor thinking fit into this book's subject of corporations, LLCs, and asset protection entities? Those same asset protection entities, when intelligently planned, can also clearly separate your investor properties from any real estate investments that might be characterized as dealer activity. There is no foolproof way to avoid being labeled a dealer if you look and act like a dealer when buying and selling a lot of properties. However, if you do the occasional fix-and-flip or subdivision and have buy-to-hold properties, using separate entities becomes critical.

Most sophisticated investors make a habit of using different entity types to separate their dealerlike activities from other real estate investments. Setting aside for the moment any discussion of the asset protection characteristics of entity choices, let's focus on the main three entity choices as they relate to separating real estate investments into dealer property and investor property categories.

S Corporations. Some would suggest that S corporations are no longer preferred for real estate investments. Not true. An S corporation is generally considered the best entity for buy-to-sell (dealer) type of properties. Why? Because of the way dealer properties are taxed, a corporation offers the benefit of the profits being passed through to the investor as profits of the corporation rather than self-employment earnings. That's an important consideration when you remember that the profits from the sale of dealer-type property in an individual's name are considered ordinary income and may trigger self-employment tax. Those same profits to an S corporation are ordinary income to the corporation, but S corporations pay no income taxes directly. Instead, all profits (after owner salaries) pass through to the shareholders as profits from the corporation. These profits that are passed through the shareholders are characterized as profit distributions not self-employment income. Minimizing self-employment income also minimizes self-employment taxes.

Limited Liability Companies. An LLC is generally considered a good entity choice for buy-to-hold (investor) type properties. The structure of an LLC is not all that different from that of an S corporation. An LLC does not pay taxes directly; rather, profits from the LLC pass through to the owners. However, the profits from an LLC may create self-employment tax issues. As such, the LLC is preferred for the buy-to-hold properties, where profits are considered and taxed as capital gains. We will discuss this issue in more detail in Chapter 6.

Limited Partnerships. Limited partnerships and family limited partnerships are considered more suitable for buy-to-hold properties for the same reasons stated above for LLCs.

Now that you know why you may need to separate dealer property from investor property, let's focus on dealer properties for a minute. Within the category of dealer property activities, you will probably want to create separate entities for each project. Why? Because it's very useful to be able to conclude a project, do the final accounting, and close up the entity. Some people make the mistake of doing multiple developments or rehabs over a number of years in the S corporation. Here's an example:

> Billie and Jenn jointly own two apartment buildings. An opportunity came along to purchase some vacant land that could be subdivided into home sites. They borrowed against the apartment buildings to buy the land. They decided to form a subchapter S corporation and construct homes on the sites. The investment went well; the following year they reinvested the subdivision profits, and their corporation took on a second project involving the construction of a small shopping center. Unfortunately, there were some problems with some of the homes they had built, and the homeowners filed a lawsuit against their corporation. Because a lawsuit had been filed against the corporation, the bank financing the shopping center development refused to extend the remaining construction funds to finish the project until the lawsuit was resolved. As a result, Billie and Jenn were forced settle what they considered to be an unreasonable lawsuit.

In the example above, Billie and Jenn did the right thing by creating an entity (subchapter S corporation) to separate their long-term investment properties from the land subdivision and houses they sold. Unfortunately, they needed to go one step further. If they had concluded the home construction project, done the final accounting, and dissolved that corporation, they could have created a new, unrelated entity for the shopping center, and the project would not have been affected by a lawsuit filed against the previous corporation. Following is a true-to-life example that illustrates this type of situation:

Jury Award: $9,760,000
Homeowners recovered for extensive damage from water intrusion and mold in their subdivision. (California, July 2005)

If the above true-to-life example had been the lawsuit filed against Billie and Jenn's corporation, it would have likely bankrupted their corporation along with their current shopping center project. If, instead, Billie and Jenn had closed the subdivision corporation and created a new corporation for the new shopping center project, the lawsuit from the earlier development would not have threatened the new project.

In the example above, the investors smartly used an S corporation for the subdivision and shopping center projects. Why was this a smart approach? It was smart because the profits from that subdivision would have been considered ordinary income. However, by using an S corporation, they could arrange for the corporation to pay them a portion of the profits in salary and the remaining profits as distributions from the corporation, thus saving some self-employment tax. Likewise, the corporation would have afforded them some tax write-offs and deferred compensation plans not available to them in the LLC entity type. As for the apartments they owned and intended to keep, an LLC is the more appropriate entity. Why? An LLC usually requires fewer formalities than a corporation, and income from rental properties is excluded from self-employment tax.

So far in this chapter, we've focused on income taxes and looked at how entities are either double-taxed or pass-through entities. We've also looked at how the taxation of real estate investments falls into two possible characterizations: investor property or dealer property. We have further considered how we might choose an appropriate asset protection entity that also allows us to separate those two types of real estate investments. Now we're going to turn our attention to the other tax considerations that impact entity choice.

State Taxes

State income taxes usually follow the federal income tax system in double-taxing corporations and some specialized trusts. So choosing the right entity to solve federal income tax problems will probably solve state income tax issues as well. However, there's another component to state taxation. Some states impose an additional tax, sometimes called an annual fee, on any entities doing business within their borders. Whatever it's called, it is still another, sometimes significant, tax that has to be paid.

For example, Table 4.1 shows California's annual fee for an LLC based on gross receipts.

California's annual fee for an LLC may not affect most real estate investors, because ongoing annual gross receipts probably fall into the first two categories. However, when an LLC sells a property, this additional tax disguised as an "annual fee" can come as quite a surprise. In many cases, a little planning can avoid this tax, but you have to be aware of it to plan for it.

Likewise, California imposes an annual tax of 1.5 percent at the entity level for S corporations, as shown in Table 4.2.

By contrast, a California limited partnership is only subject to an $800 flat tax annually. So if you were developing or subdividing land for resale with anticipated profits in the million-dollar range, choosing a limited partnership entity form over an LLC or an S corporation would save you $6,000 to $15,000. Each state is different, so you will want to be aware of how your state taxes the different entities you may be considering.

Estate Tax–Planning Considerations

Yet another tax factor is estate tax planning. In some cases, clients are not primarily motivated by asset protection considerations. Instead, their entity needs are based on a desire to start passing ownership of assets to the next generation while they are still alive. There can be a lot of reasons for this strategy, but the main one is usually estate tax

TABLE 4.1 *California's LLC Fee Structure*

Total Income from All Sources	Annual Fee
From $0 but less than $249,999	$800
$250,000 or more but less than $499,999	$900
$500,000 or more but less than $999,999	$2,500
$1,000,000 or more but less than $4,999,999	$6,000
$5,000,000 or more	$11,790

TABLE 4.2 *California's S Corporation Fee Structure*

S Corporation Net Income	Tax Rate	Tax Due
$50,000	1.5%	$750
$75,000	1.5%	$1,125
$100,000	1.5%	$1,500
$150,000	1.5%	$2,250
$200,000	1.5%	$3,000
$300,000	1.5%	$4,500
$400,000	1.5%	$6,000
$500,000	1.5%	$7,500
$800,000	1.5%	$12,000
$1,000,000	1.5%	$15,000

avoidance. If your estate is large enough, then this might be on your mind. The estate tax exemption as this book goes to press is $2 million per person. Table 4.3 shows current and future estate and gift tax rates as written in current federal law.

If a husband and wife have an $8 million estate, they have a problem. Some people would say that's a good problem to have, but it's a problem nonetheless. If both of them die in 2008, $4 million can pass to their heirs

TABLE 4.3 *Estate and Gift Taxes*

Year	Estate Tax Exemption	Gift Tax Exemption	Highest Estate and Gift Tax Rate
2008	$2 million	$1 million	45%
2009	$3.5 million	$1 million	45%
2010	Estate tax repealed	$1 million	45% (gift tax only)
2011	$1 million	$1 million	55%

without any estate taxes, but the other $4 million will incur stiff estate taxes. As you can see from Table 4.3, estate tax rates are generally about 45 percent. In our $8 million estate example, that's about $1.8 million in estate taxes. Obviously, this couple would be looking for ways to avoid this outcome.

You can try to find an entity style that will allow you to gift a certain amount of ownership of the entity to your children on a systematic basis. This depletes that $8 million a little bit at a time until it is more manageable. Our present system for estate tax exemptions is stepping up to a higher exemption every few years but is set to drop back down to $1 million per person in 2011. Also, a tremendous effort is underway in Congress to pass legislation to set a permanent estate tax exemption amount. With these variables in mind, it is hard to establish a long-term plan when you do not know what the estate tax exemption will be even a few years from now. If you do all this gifting and then the exemption goes up to $5 million per person, and you only had $8 million to begin with, you have just gone though a whole bunch of effort and significantly complicated your life for no benefit. Obviously, this uncertainty deters some people from doing this type of gifting.

On the flip side, making the effort can easily pay off, because over a period of time, you can gift a lot of money. Imagine that you are in the $8 million category and the exemption is a total of $4 million. Unfortunately, both you and your spouse die in a car accident. If you gifted away

$2 million before your untimely death, then only $2 million is estate taxable, and you have effectively saved your kids $1 million in taxes that otherwise would have gone to the IRS. That savings is certainly worth the effort. So when you are looking at forming entities, family ownership and estate planning considerations come into play as well. It is a good idea to have a conversation with your estate-planning attorney to see whether forming an entity for gifting purposes fits your situation.

If estate tax planning is a very important component of your entity choice, a family limited partnership might be a good choice. Family limited partnerships can be fairly complicated and sometimes expensive to implement, but the potential for state tax savings may be significant enough to make it all worthwhile. We'll be taking a closer look at family limited partnerships in Chapter 8.

Property Transfer Requirements and Pitfalls

The final taxation consideration that has to be factored in is property taxes. Property taxes are sometimes affected by transferring real estate into or out of an entity. In many counties, certain transfers of real estate trigger a reassessment valuation for property tax purposes. It's important to know if transferring your real estate into an entity will result in higher taxes. Most counties have an exemption for transfers of property into or out of entities where the underlying owners remain the same. Generally, pass-through entities, such as partnerships or LLCs, do not trigger a reassessment. However, transfers into more complex entities with multiple owners are more likely to cause problems. Steering clear of these problems is important, because once a property is reassessed, the higher tax value is very difficult to undo. Property tax implications should always be discussed with an attorney before a transfer is made.

In states like California, planners have to be especially sensitive to reassessment issues. Making a mistake that triggers a reassessment can easily end up costing the property owner tens of thousands of dollars in

TABLE 4.4 *Entity Type Comparison*

	Sole Proprietorship	Partnership	Limited Partnership	C Corporation	S Corporation	LLC	Series LLC
Formation Complexity	Very Low	Low	Medium	Very High	Very High	High	High
Cost of Formation	Very Low	Low	Medium	High	High	High	High
Liability for Principles	100% Liable	100% Liable	Gen. Partner Liable/ Lim. Partner has Lim. Liability	Limited Liability	Limited Liability	Limited Liability	Limited Liability
Must File Entity Tax Return?	No	Yes	Yes	Yes	Yes	Yes	Yes
Are Taxes "Passed Through"?	Yes	Yes	Yes	No	Yes	Yes	Yes
Stock Issuance Considerations?	No	No	No	Yes	Yes	No	No
Yearly Administrative Burden	Very Low	Low	Low	High	High	Medium	High
Continues on Perpetually?	No	No	No	Yes	Yes	Yes	Yes
Available in All States?	Yes	Yes	Yes	Yes	Yes	Yes	No
Different Business Ventures Allowed under One Entity?	No	No	No	No	No	No	Yes

additional property taxes. Usually, county assessor rules establish which transfers are exempt from reassessment. You want to make sure your advisor knows and stays within those rules.

Summary

A lot of tax considerations need to go into choosing an entity type. For real estate investors, some are more important than others. Are you considering a pass-through entity? Are you a property dealer or a property investor? Do you need more than one entity to separate different types of real estate investments? Do you need to plan for estate taxes? Will transferring a property into the entity you've chosen cause an increase in your property taxes? All of these tax questions are important in deciding your entity type, and they should be considered together to find a balance that fits your particular needs.

These tax factors need to be considered together with the other factors listed in Chapter 3 to decide what entity type provides the best balance for your situation. Table 4.4 summarizes some of these factors.

5 Corporations

CORPORATIONS OFFER EXCELLENT liability-limiting characteristics for shareholders (owners) but provide very little protection from outside liabilities. For this reason, the use of corporations is really limited to active real estate business ventures like subdivisions, rehab projects, and multiple homebuilding developments. As we'll see, corporations are well suited for these types of projects, because they offer tax benefits and deferred compensation possibilities more closely associated with active businesses.

Why Subchapter S Corporations Are Better: Taxation Pros and Cons

Up to this point, we have touched on corporations from a number of different perspectives. In this chapter, we will take a closer look at the mechanics of forming and using a corporation. The obvious advantage of incorporating is that the corporation shareholders are completely protected from the liabilities of the corporation. Likewise, the directors and officers of the corporation are protected from its liabilities. However, directors and officers of a corporation can be held liable for their actions in situations of fraud or criminal activity. Setting that aside, a large body of well-established law pretty much makes it certain that officers, directors, and shareholders are completely protected from the liabilities of the corporation.

So what type of corporation is best? We've already determined that there are different types of corporations: C corporations, S corporations, professional corporations, and nonprofit corporations. For real estate investments, we can quickly rule out professional corporations. Also, nonprofit corporations have some specialty uses in real estate investments, but their rarity excludes them from the scope of this book. That leaves us with the main two corporate types: the S corporation and the C corporation. In both cases, the liability protection for the shareholders, officers, and directors is pretty much identical. The main difference between the two, as we have mentioned briefly already, is how they are taxed. The C corporation is not a pass-through entity, so its profits are subject to double taxation. It must file a tax return and pay taxes at the corporate level. After it has paid the corporate taxes, it distributes the after-tax dollars in the form of dividends to the shareholders, who then file their personal income tax returns and pay taxes on those dividends. Because of this double taxation, we can usually rule out the C corporation for real estate investments.

An S corporation is a special form of corporation. The *S* refers to subchapter S of the tax code. S corporations are based on the same structure as C corporations, but they are not double taxed. Instead, the income of an S corporation is "passed through" to the personal income of its shareholders in proportion to their ownership interest. This tax structure makes the S corporation very favorable for some real estate investment ventures.

An S corporation starts out as a traditional C corporation, and then, by filing the IRS Form 2553 (the subchapter S election), it converts to an S corporation. The subchapter S election usually must be made by filing the appropriate form within 75 days of when the corporation begins conducting business as a corporation, issues stock to shareholders, or acquires assets.

Additionally, certain restrictions must be complied with to qualify for the subchapter S election. Some of those restrictions include the following:

- S corporations cannot have more than 100 shareholders.
- All shareholders must be individuals, not other entities.
- All shareholders must be U.S. citizens or U.S. residents.
- S corporations may have only one class of stock.

Setting aside those restrictions, the S corporation structure is very similar to that of a C corporation; the formalities, the officers, the directors, all of the internal formation documents, the internal operating guidelines, and the bylaws are virtually identical between the S and the C corporation.

Formalities of Formation

Articles of Incorporation

Some fairly rigid formalities must be followed to create and maintain a valid corporation. Each state has its own corporate filing rules and annual formalities that must be observed, so depending on where you choose to incorporate, you'll need to look at that state's specific detailed guidelines. Although state rules vary, one thing they all have in common is a requirement that you record, or file, a document referred to as the *articles of incorporation*.

The articles of incorporation simply set out some basic information of the corporation. For example, articles of incorporation would include the following:

- The new corporation's name and initial address or principal place of business

- The corporate purpose, usually something like "to engage in any lawful activity" or some similar language acceptable to the state
- Name and address of the corporation's registered agent for service of process
- Stock information, including number of shares the corporation is authorized to issue, a designation of classes of shares, if any, and the value of each share
- The name and address of the incorporator of the new corporation

It is usually desirable to keep the provisions set out in the articles of incorporation short and very general in nature so that the articles do not limit the corporation from engaging in different types of business activities.

The person who is incorporating the corporation may or may not be one of the owners. In fact, if you use an attorney to help you form your corporation, the attorney will be your incorporator.

An agent for service of process is required, because upon filing the articles of incorporation, you have created an independent entity that has the ability to own property and conduct business. This new, independent entity must name a real, or "natural," person for the purpose of receiving correspondence from government agencies and service of process from the court system. Your designated agent could be a director of the corporation, it could be someone else you hire, or it could even be another corporation that is registered with the state to provide that type of service. As with the incorporator, if you have an attorney create your corporation, the initial agent for service of process likely will be that attorney.

Once you have your articles of incorporation drafted, they must be filed. How long it actually takes to get articles of incorporation filed and validated varies from state to state. In California, generally speaking, the time needed to form a corporation is two to three business days. The California Department of Corporations' official time estimate says filing takes much longer, but there are ways to cut the time down significantly. In my practice, it generally takes two to three business days to be up and running with filed and validated articles of incorporation.

Once the articles of incorporation have been filed and validated, the next step is for the person who incorporated the new corporation to resign, thus turning over control of the new corporation to its owner(s) who will act as the initial director(s). This step is just a formality, but it must be documented. At that point, some of the structure of the corporation needs to be established. This is accomplished by having the initial meeting, also known as the organizational meeting.

The Organizational Meeting

As soon as the incorporator resigns and the first director(s) gain control of the corporation, the director(s) must hold an organizational meeting. This meeting has a number of items on the agenda, all which must be addressed for the corporation to fulfill its formal requirements. The decisions made in this meeting are documented in the *minutes of the meeting,* or "minutes" for short. The minutes become the official proof or paper trail that establishes the fact that certain formalities were observed and the corporation structure acts independently of the owners of the corporation.

It's sometimes difficult to imagine the need for this level of formality in a small corporation structure. Nevertheless, it is required, and skipping these formalities will seriously jeopardize the effectiveness of your corporate structure. Along those lines, it seems almost absurd to have a "meeting" and document decisions when a single individual owns 100 percent of the corporation. But again, the formalities must be followed. Using an attorney, the organizational meeting is usually just a short appointment at the attorney's office. Most of the work will already be done for you, and your time will be spent signing documents. Below, we will look at the types of things that need to be accomplished in this organizational meeting.

Bylaws. The first item on the agenda of the organizational meeting is to adopt a set of bylaws. This is generally pretty straightforward, because the bylaws of a corporation are fairly standardized unless your corporation has unusual needs. The bylaws provide most of the organizational structure for the corporation. They say what type of officers there will be (president, secretary, treasurer, etc.), what those officers are responsible for, when the annual meetings will be held, and many other structural provisions. The bylaws dictate how the corporation will conduct itself.

I want to take a minute to explain the difference between the bylaws and the minutes, because confusion sometimes occurs. The minutes are updated annually, whereas the bylaws, while they can be amended, are not meant to be a fluid document. You set up your relatively rigid structure with the bylaws and then fill that structure with the minutes. Any and all changes that may happen year to year are variable, but they still have to fall within the structure that was created in the bylaws. For example, say your bylaws state that you must have two directors. Each year, there must be two directors, but Year 1's directors might be Bob and Susan, while Year 2's directors might be Frank and Jill. The change is listed in the minutes.

Appointment of Officers. Once the bylaws have been adopted establishing the number of officers that will direct the corporation, the next job is for the director(s) to appoint or name the persons who will fill the positions. The reason for formally appointing or naming officers is to make it clear who is in charge and has authority to act on behalf of the corporation. Now, if just you and your spouse own the corporation, is it really necessary to designate which one of you will hold which offices? Yes, it is necessary. You may each take on a few different offices, but those must be documented. Why? Because as you go about doing things for this corporation, people will ask for documentation that shows who has the authority to act on behalf of the corporation. If you do not designate the positions of authority and appoint someone to fill those positions, how can anyone know that you have any authority to act? For example, without proper documentation, you would not be able to open a bank account or sign checks. This brings us to the next item that needs to be accomplished in the organizational meeting: banking authorizations.

Banking Authorization. Following your appointment of officers, the directors need to establish which officers are authorized to conduct banking activities. Usually, the first thing most people want to do is open a bank account for the corporation. The person who goes into the bank to open that account will need the following:

- An original copy of the articles of incorporation as proof that the corporation actually exists under the laws of the state
- A banking resolution to show that she is the person authorized to conduct banking activities on behalf of the corporation
- An employer identification number (EIN), or tax ID number (Getting your tax ID number happens after the organizational meeting, so we will discuss it more in just a minute.)

With these things in hand, you'll be able to open a business account on behalf of the corporation.

This may sound complicated, but in reality, the banking resolution is simply contained in the minutes of the first meeting. If you have an attorney form your new corporation for you, all of these necessary items will be provided to you via a corporate records binder you receive from your lawyer's office. Just take that corporate record binder to the bank, and you will have everything they will ask for.

Stock Issuance Considerations. The last major item on the organizational meeting's agenda is to complete and issue stock certificates, which represent the ownership of the corporation. Stock certificates are pretty common items, but filling them out properly can be tricky. Obviously, because the stock certificates represent the ownership of the corporation, it's very important that issuing them is done correctly. How much stock is issued to each shareholder is a matter of how many people are involved and what each person's contributions are. If one individual owns the entire corporation, obviously all the stock will be issued to that person. Once the shareholders are determined and the formality of issuing the stock has been completed, this action will also be documented in the minutes of the organizational meeting.

After the Organizational Meeting

At the end of the organizational meeting, the corporation has a set of documents that include the articles of incorporation and the minutes of the meeting. These two documents, along with the issued stock certificates, tie everything together and document that the corporation (a) incorporated properly with the state, (b) adopted bylaws giving it a recognized business structure to allow it to do business, and (c) commenced doing business by appointing officers and authorizing certain officers to conduct banking activities on behalf of the corporation.

Even when the organizational meeting is concluded, some more steps must be taken immediately to complete the process. Once the shell of the corporation is evident in the form of the articles and the organizational meeting has established the officers, the very next action is to file for an employer's identification number (EIN). As mentioned previously, an EIN number is also referred to as a tax ID number. They are one and the same. Filing for and receiving the corporation's tax ID number must be done as soon as possible, because the tax ID number, as stated earlier, is required to open a bank account.

Additionally, the corporation must file the S election (IRS Form 2553: "Election for Small Business Corporations") if it wishes to be an S corporation and, therefore, a pass-through entity. This is also just a matter of filing a form, but it needs to be filed by an officer of the corporation in his authorized capacity; therefore, the corporation cannot file the S election until *after* officers have been appointed.

Next, the corporation must determine who the ongoing agent for service of process will be. The ongoing agent for service of process can be the same as the initial one, but that decision must be made.

Also, the state will require a couple of things of the corporation. The rules obviously vary a little from state to state, but you likely will need to file a statement of information with the state to tell it who has been authorized to act on behalf of the corporation, who the directors are, who the officers are, etc. Remember, when the articles of incorporation were originally filed, those things were not yet decided. The articles of incorporation just said who the incorporator was, who the initial agent for service of process was, and that the corporation was being created to do business. Once all the other things have been decided, you have to go back and provide the updated information to the state where you have incorporated. In California, for example, you would be required to file a statement of information within 90 days of filing the articles of incorporation (and annually thereafter). Every state has some similar requirement.

Just about everything you need to do when creating a corporation has a deadline associated with it. You have only a certain amount of time to complete all the filing requirements. If you don't complete the formation requirements in a timely manner, or disregard some of the actions necessary to establish a corporation as a separate entity, you open yourself up to the possibility that a court may set aside your corporate structure. The last thing you want to have happen is a situation where a lawsuit has arisen and your protective entity doesn't hold up because you overlooked some of the required formalities.

This whole start-up process may sound burdensome, but for somebody like an attorney who does this for a living, it is fairly straightforward. Refer to Figure 5.1 to see a flow chart of the incorporation process. Once your corporation is properly formed and the initial round of deadlines is met, the paperwork drops off considerably, and any future paperwork is generally required only once a year.

FIGURE 5.1 *Flow Chart of the Incorporation Process*

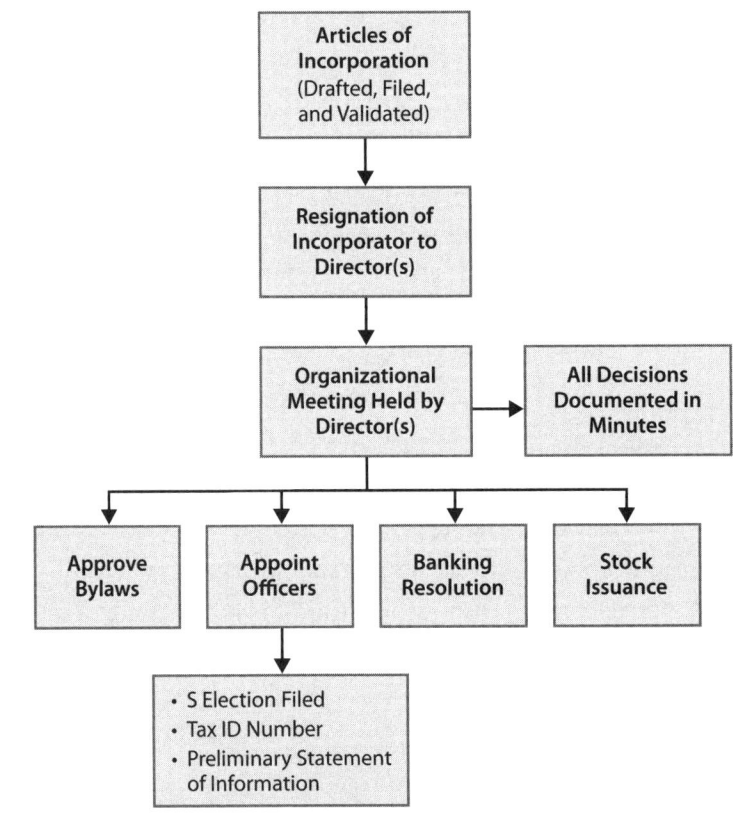

The Resulting Hierarchy

At this point, we have talked about how directors, officers, and shareholders come into being. All of that gets a little confusing sometimes, so let's spend a minute and look at the ongoing hierarchy that will exist within a corporation. This hierarchy starts with the shareholders of a corporation, who vote in or appoint the directors on a normal ongoing basis. The directors then appoint the officers of the corporation. In other words, officers of the corporation report to the directors, the directors are responsible to the shareholders, and

FIGURE 5.2 *Corporation Hierarchy Flow Chart*

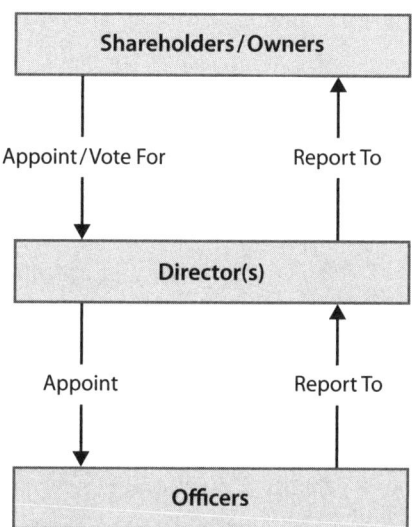

shareholders presumably have the ultimate power. Refer to Figure 5.2 to see this hierarchy illustrated.

The structure of corporations is long established, and how things are done is pretty well set in stone. One of the major things that is always scrutinized when a question of shareholder liability arises is whether the corporate formalities were observed and whether the corporation was actually acting as an independent entity. If the formalities were not observed and a determination is made that the corporation was not independent of its shareholders, your asset protections will fail you when you need them most.

Cardboard Corporations

I was in Las Vegas right around the time the famous Excalibur Casino had its grand opening. This huge, castlelike building was an amazing sight at the time. As we were headed there, the taxi driver told us that the local residents referred to it as "Cardboard Castle." When we got there, I understood what he was talking about. From a distance, it looked like this huge, solid, stone castle with larger-than-life statues and medieval shields on the wall. But once I got up close, I realized that the solid stone exterior and shields were fake. In fact, most of the exterior appearance was just styrofoam and plywood props. Up close, you could see the facade really had no substance at all.

I think the term *cardboard corporation* is especially descriptive when thinking about how some people go about forming and operating their corporations (or other entities). Just like the Cardboard Castle in Las Vegas used a bunch of cheap shortcuts to appear to be made solidly, so do cardboard corporations. Some people think it's easier to take shortcuts and avoid the required formalities. In short, it's easier just to "look" like a corporation. For those people, what they have created is really just a cardboard corporation that lacks substance and is easily knocked aside the first time it's attacked. Some people create cardboard corporations by taking shortcuts right from the beginning. Others start out with a solid corporation but get lazy and let it become a cardboard corporation through neglect. Whatever the reason, a cardboard corporation offers the illusion of liability shield but won't really provide any protection when needed.

Costs to Create and Operate
Using an Attorney to Form Your Corporation

Because the formality requirements are so high and so many steps are necessary to set up a valid corporation, it is usually advisable to have an attorney do it for you. Filing the necessary paperwork with your state's department of corporations is just the start. You also have to maneuver through the new-entity paperwork required by the IRS and your state's taxation board. Likewise, if you've never done an organizational meeting, drafted bylaws, recorded minutes, or issued stock certificates, it can all be a little mind-boggling.

With that in mind, the question becomes: how do you get all this stuff done? The costs to create a corporation will vary depending on how you go about it, but surprisingly they do not vary that much. Whether you hire an attorney or decide on some other seemingly less expensive method of incorporating, by the time everything is said and done, you will either have spent close to the same amount of money or you will have taken on a tremendous amount of work yourself.

As an attorney, my advice is obviously to avoid attempting this stuff yourself; pay an attorney who does this every day to do it for you correctly. I know that sounds self-serving, but consider this: as a real estate investor, the first corporation I ever formed was done by another lawyer whom I hired. He was not a friend or an associate; in fact, I had never met him before. Why would a lawyer hire another lawyer? At that time, I didn't specialize in entity formation, so I wanted somebody who worked in this area every day to make sure it was done right. I suggest you do the same.

With that said, let's look at using an attorney to form your corporation. Attorneys come in many shapes and sizes and with many different professional philosophies—and by that, I mean prices. Some attorneys are very expensive, and others seem almost suspiciously inexpensive. The difference between them sometimes is an unknown factor. Is it worth spending $500 an hour on the hot shot from the big city, or will the guy down the road do as good a job for $200 an hour? Unfortunately, at first glance, there is no way to know. The best place to start is by trying to figure out if somebody you know has used an attorney for the same services. This way, you can get a referral to that attorney and know before you make the phone call whether the attorney is somebody you could consider doing business with. There are also a lot of attorney referral services out there, but I would not suggest using a referral service unless you absolutely trust it. Most of these referral services check no qualifications whatsoever; their participating attorneys simply pay a certain amount of money to be listed as an attorney in a particular field.

Another course of action, of course, is to compare rates. Different attorneys charge different amounts for the same services. Sometimes the variation between two attorneys can be huge, even though they seem to have the same qualifications and do the same things. Likewise, some attorneys charge for everything by the hour, while other charge flat rates for certain services.

One thing to keep in mind is that attorneys are specialists. If you have a friend of a friend who's a family law lawyer, and she offers to do your corporation for you, I would suggest you find a polite way to decline. What that person doesn't know *will* hurt you. Attorneys, like everyone else, get used to seeing and solving certain problems. There is a learning curve. Just because a person is a lawyer doesn't mean he knows anything about the process and formalities of creating corporations. So don't let that friend-of-a-friend lawyer do your corporation for you. The best choice is to go to an attorney who specializes in the creation of entities, corporations, and LLCs as part of everyday practice.

Using Online Corporation Formation Services

Complying with all the formalities required to form a corporation (or any other entity) can't be accomplished with a few clicks of your mouse. As you have seen, there's much more to creating and maintaining a corporation than just filing a piece of paper with the state. Nevertheless, if you go on the Internet, you will find literally hundreds of companies that say they will incorporate your business for you. Each one of them makes it sound as if all you have to do is pay a few hundred dollars, file some papers, and be done. The only thing these companies do, though, is file your articles of incorporation and then hand everything off to you to finish. Remember, filing the articles of incorporation is only one of many steps. The staff at these services are not lawyers, so they are not allowed to advise you on how best to structure your corporation, how to complete the bylaws, what needs to be documented in the minutes of the organizational meeting, or how to issue stock to the shareholders of the corporation. All of these things involve the practice of law, and advice can only be given by lawyers.

I would encourage you to go ahead and take a look at some of these Internet incorporation companies just so you can see what they offer compared to what you actually have to do to have a working, valid corporation. You will find that what they do for their "special deal" price is send a one-page, generic articles of incorporation to the state to be stamped by the state clerk. That's about 5 percent of the whole process, and you can do that yourself with an envelope and a postage stamp. What they don't do (or tell you about) is everything else that needs to be done so that your corporation actually protects you. Earlier in this chapter, we looked at the definition of a "cardboard corporation." That's exactly what these online companies sell you, a corporation that lacks the substance needed to protect you from lawsuits.

The pricing strategy that they advertise makes their service seem too good to be true, which it is. Some of the online sites actually look pretty convincing. Some, for an additional fee, will even offer to file some of the other state or federal paperwork for you. They'll call it the "Gold Package" or the "Premium Package," and you can check boxes for which papers you would like them to file on your behalf. The list of services looks impressive, so I imagine most people are fooled into thinking that if they check all the boxes for the "Complete Package," then they're all done. But in reality, even the "Complete Package" offered by online corporations is not going to withstand a lawsuit. Why? Because no matter how complete these companies' make their services look, they are not staffed by attorneys and cannot advise you on what steps to take after your papers are filed. They cannot help you properly structure the minutes of your organizational meeting. They can't help you with banking resolutions, or annual meeting requirements, or the importance of properly planning and issuing stock.

The fact is, most people don't really understand what's involved, so they go ahead and use these online services. They think they're all done, but a few months later, they start getting letters from a bunch of different government entities talking about forms that need to be submitted, deadlines that have to be met, and penalties for noncompliance. They're getting all those letters because their online service didn't comply with all the state regulations and didn't tell them that someone had to do it. Even though they may have paid for the "Gold Package" or the "Complete Set," they soon find out that there is more to it than what the online marketing company told them. When they realize that they have created a mess and finally call an attorney to get help, the attorney basically has to start over. The filed articles of incorporation are usually valid, but in most cases, everything else needs to be professionally redrafted or redone. And here is the real kicker: after the client checked all the boxes for the "Gold Package" or "Complete Set," they probably ended up paying as much as they would if they'd simply had an attorney do it right to begin with.

Hopefully you can see the problem with the online incorporation companies. Their Web sites are designed to seem professional, and their services seem convenient, but their marketing is designed to lure in people who really don't understand the process. They're looking for that person who will plop down a credit card, thinking she's found some secret shortcut. Those online services don't expect ever to hear from you again. To add insult to injury, when you sign up for their services, you also contractually agree that they will not be responsible for any mistakes or problems that arise from *your* incorporation. If you read their disclaimers, you will find statements such as the following in the fine print.

> Our services are not intended to replace the advice of an attorney. . . . All services are provided as-is with no representations or warranties. . . . You assume complete responsibility and risk for use of this site and any/all site-related services. . . . By using this service, you waive any rights or claims you may have. . . . We are not a law firm, and our employees are not acting as your attorney; instead,

you are representing yourself and are solely responsible. . . . This Web site is not a substitute for the advice of an attorney. . . . You should consult a licensed attorney in your area. . . . The information provided by this Web site is not guaranteed to be correct, complete, or up-to-date. . . . You agree that you have been advised of the possibility of loss or damage and hereby waive any and all claims. . . .

Why would you pay hundreds of dollars for a service that claims no responsibility, leaves you out in the cold, and cannot even guarantee that your documents comply with current laws? Contrast that with hiring an attorney. An attorney assumes you will have future questions and he will to see you again. Attorneys are always accountable for the service they provide. If there is a problem with the corporation, if you need changes to it, or if anything comes up that you don't understand, it's nice to know there'll be an attorney who can answer your questions. If you refer to Figure 5.3, you will see what parts of the process the online companies actually provide and how their services compare to what an attorney provides.

Everybody likes to save money, but as you'll see from Table 5.1, you "save" only a few hundred dollars by taking online shortcuts over having an attorney do it right. Asset protection is all about trying to reduce risks. I'll never understand why people are willing to risk taking shortcuts.

Incorporation Do-It-Yourself Books and Kits

A number of publications and form-your-own-corporation kits are available in bookstores, online, through Amazon.com, and through other sources. While the sales material on the back of those books and kits makes it seem as if incorporating is very simple, again I cannot stress enough that if you do not know what you are doing, you will very likely make costly mistakes. It really is worth your time, effort, and money to hire an attorney and make sure you complete the process properly. If you are either well versed in corporation formation or have a tremendous amount of time on your hands and wish to learn how to

FIGURE 5.3 *Online Companies' Services*

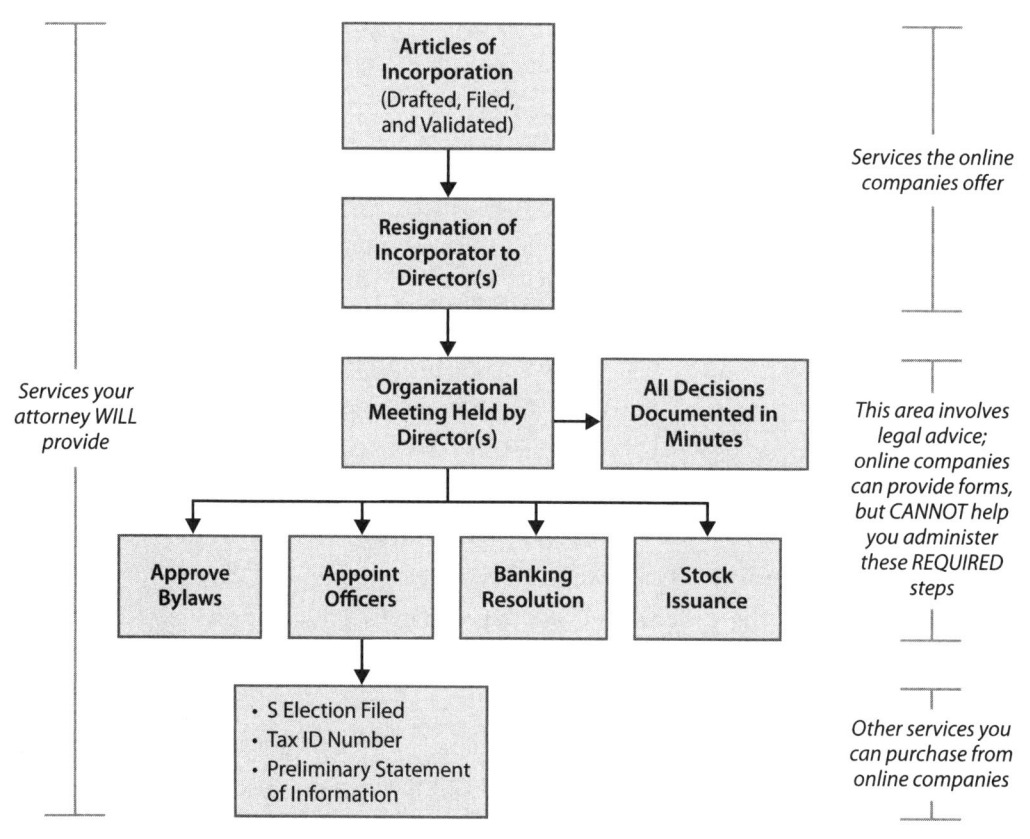

do all this (and don't mind being frustrated with the mistakes that you'll make along the way), then I suppose one of those books or kits might be for you. Most of my clients, however, value their time and would prefer not to have to learn how to do this the hard way; they would rather have somebody form their corporation for them so that the structure is in place and up and running correctly.

This is especially true in situations involving real estate. There are a couple of taxation aspects of holding real estate in a corporation that those books and kits don't talk about. They are not about the taxation of

TABLE 5.1 *Comparison of Online Service and Attorney's Service*

	Leading Online Company Basic Package ($150)	Attorney ($1,000)
Preliminary Name Search	✓	✓
Preparation and Filing Articles of Incorporation	✓	✓
Bylaws Form	✓	✓
Bylaws Completed and Validated	Not Provided	✓
Resolutions Drafted	Not Provided	✓
Stock Certificates Provided	✓	✓
Stock Issuance	Not Provided	✓
Corporate Kit (includes binder and seal)	$100	✓
Minutes Form	✓	✓
Minutes Completed and Validated	Not Provided	✓
Tax ID Number	$70	✓
Prepare S Election	$70	✓
Obtain S Status from IRS	Not Provided	✓
Statement of Information	$100	✓
Conduct Organizational Meeting*	Not Provided	✓
Deeding Property**	Not Provided	✓
Five to Ten Business Day Service	$150	✓
Legal Advice on All Steps of the Process, Taking into Account Individual Nuances	Not Provided	✓
All Forms Completed for You, with No Time Spent Figuring Out the Process	Not Provided	✓
Registered Agent for First Year	$160	✓
Shipping and Handling for Your Documents	$20	✓
Person with Legal Responsibility for Errors***	YOU	ATTORNEY
Actual Cost (not including state filing fees)	$820	$1,000 (Sometimes this includes state fees.)

* Required for proper formation but not provided AT ALL by online services.
** Has SERIOUS tax implications but not provided AT ALL by online services.
*** This item alone could be worth thousands of dollars and should negate any difference in start-up costs.

Notice that certain items are REQUIRED but not offered at all by online companies. You either have to figure them out yourself or hire an attorney anyway. By using an attorney, not only do you get these additional items but you get peace of mind; with the online companies, you get, at best, a false sense of security.

corporations; instead, they are about the simple act of filing the articles of incorporation. Again, there is no substitute for getting the proper advice. Remember that if you take the road of books, kits, or online corporation formation, an attorney will usually refuse to work on documents that were incorrectly filed or drafted if you need that attorney's help down the road.

Yearly Tax Returns, State Fees, and Other Expected Fees

We have discussed what you can expect to pay for creating a corporation; now we will discuss the items you can expect to pay for on an ongoing basis. The first is the cost of having tax returns filed for the corporation on an annual basis. You may not have corporate taxes if the corporation is an S corporation, but you still have to file the returns. This means paying an accountant if you do not want to deal with filing the returns yourself. If the venture is ongoing, there will be salaries for employees and other things that involve payroll considerations. Additionally, there are some minimal banking charges for commercial bank accounts. Also, many states charge an annual fee for creating the corporation structure in that state. For example, California's Franchise Tax Board charges a minimum tax whether the corporation had a profit or did absolutely nothing during the year. The fact that structure exists under the California infrastructure justifies the Franchise Tax Board to tax a minimum of $800 per year, per corporation. Further, the department of corporations in your state likely requires annual updates for the corporation that cost a fee to file. Finally, you can expect to pay your agent for service of process if you hired someone or a company specifically to perform that duty (rather than naming yourself as the agent for service of process).

Sometimes these ongoing costs are not really significant, but they can become significant if you have a number of entities going at the same time. The costs for multiple entities can easily add up. It is worth your time to look into the costs involved and have an idea of what to expect.

Why You Should Consider Hiring an Agent for Service of Process

I have mentioned the agent for service of process a couple of times. First, I mentioned it because you are required to list one for your articles of incorporation as a formality of formation. Second, the agent was mentioned above because it can cost your corporation money on a regular basis. We know that you must have an agent for service of process so the state, the IRS, and other agencies know with whom to correspond regarding the corporation. Can you be the agent for service of process for your own corporation? You certainly can. There are no rules against that. However, take into consideration that the agent's name is public information. Sometimes it is not easy to find who owns a corporation, but it is always easy to find the agent for service of process. Usually, all you have to do is go online and search for the company on the state's corporations Web site, and the agent for service of process will appear right there with the rest of the public information for that company.

There are two reasons why this may be important. First is a privacy concern. Many of my clients don't maintain a separate office, so they don't like the idea that their home address is going to be a matter of public record. If an attorney is looking for the owner of a corporation and you as a shareholder or owner of the corporation are listed, then it can be very easy for that attorney to cross-reference you to other assets you might own. All of a sudden, you are very exposed, and you lose a huge part of your privacy.

Second, when attorneys are first considering whether filing a lawsuit against a corporation will be worthwhile, one of the things they look at is how well you followed the corporate formalities. In other words, did you do everything properly so that your corporate entity will actually protect you or bar them from being able to come after your personal assets? The first clue they can get in this regard is who is listed as your agent for service of process. If you and your home address are listed or if you have listed some dot-com company as the agent, this information indicates that a lawyer is not advising you. As such, there is a much higher probability that your corporate shell can be attacked and may not be able to protect your assets. Why would anyone want to expose themselves that way? If, on the other hand, your listed agent is your *attorney-at-law*, it sends a whole different message. Now the presumption is that you did not take any shortcuts and that your corporation will, in fact, protect your personal assets from attack.

Transferring Property into or out of a Corporation

Transferring property into or out of a corporation requires multifaceted analysis. Most of your considerations are tax related, yet some concern mortgages as well as insurance. Assuming that the corporation has been formed properly and that all the required documents are in place to support the corporation's validity, then transferring property into the corporation becomes a matter of steering clear of taxation, mortgage, and insurance problems.

How does the transfer of properties into or out of a corporation incur tax consequences? Transferring property into a corporation generally does not cause problems with state or federal income tax or capital gains taxes—but taking it out generally does. You have to be aware of when you can take it out and how to do it without triggering taxation or causing some other problem. Property taxes are another issue. In many states, if you transfer a property at all, it can trigger a property tax reassessment. Most states will not reassess the property if it is shown that the owners of the corporation are the same as the owners of the property before the transfer. Also, if the transfer is just into an entity where all the owners own an equal amount, then the state will likely not reassess the property. In other words, they will disregard the transfer and presume that the ownership has not changed; the only thing that has changed is the *form* of ownership. That is important, because inadvertently triggering a reassessment of property taxes sometimes takes a couple of years in the appeals process to get reversed. It is one of those problems that you really want to steer clear of.

Most properties have some type of mortgage on them, so the mortgage is a concern as well. Most mortgage notes or trust deeds have provisions in them that are called *due-on-sale* or *due-on-transfer clauses*. Basically, such a clause states that if the property is transferred or sold, the lending institution has the right to call that note due and payable in full. In many situations, that would be disastrous. The proper way to approach the situation, of course, is to contact the bank, let it know what you are doing, and make sure it does not have an objection to your transferring the property into an entity for liability or asset protection purposes. Most lending institutions do not have a problem, but not asking first is risky and could have dire consequences.

Presumably, if you own a piece of property that you are considering transferring into an entity, you already have property and title insurance of some kind. When you transfer that property, you are no longer the owner of that property; your corporation is the owner. If the owner is now different, both the property and title insurance may no longer apply. Therefore, it is prudent to have a conversation with your insurance company (just as with your lending institution) to make sure it has no objections to the transfer. If it does, then you will likely need to name the corporation as an additional insured. The process is fairly straightforward, but not doing so can mean disaster.

Dealing with Government Agencies

All business entities have to interact with many different government agencies. It doesn't matter if your entity is a corporation, an LLC, a limited partnership, or something else. If it's a separate business entity, it must file various annual reports, tax forms, and any other paperwork the government requires of that entity type. Sometimes, this paperwork may seem a bit out of hand. Nevertheless, it's important that you meet all the requirements and file everything necessary to maintain the integrity of your business entity. As you'll see later, these compliance issues will be scrutinized closely in determining whether your corporation can protect you from liability. The logic: if you don't follow requirements of maintaining a valid corporation, then why should the courts enforce your right to use it as a shield?

Many people are simply not good at maintaining required paperwork. If that's you, then you seriously may want to consider hiring your lawyer's office or an independent corporate service company to handle required paperwork for you.

Using Corporate Compliance Services

We just talked about the importance of filing the annual reports and other government forms necessary to maintain the integrity of your corporation or other entity. A number of internal formalities of the corporation also must be fulfilled on a yearly basis. As we said, your lawyer's office probably provides this service, but there are also companies that just do corporate compliance work. Whether provided by a lawyer's office or one of the corporate compliance companies, this service is usually not very expensive, and it takes a lot of the burden off your shoulders. More importantly, regularly meeting all your requirements strongly supports the structure and asset protection features of your entity. As you'll see from the next section, failure to fulfill these requirements is one of the main reasons courts set aside entity protections and allow creditors to go after personal assets.

Piercing the Corporate Veil

The primary reason to create a corporation or any other asset protection entity is to limit the liability of the owners and/or to protect assets in the entity. However, under certain circumstances, the courts will impose liability on the individual owners for the debts of the corporation. This concept is commonly referred to as *piercing the corporate veil* or *disregarding the corporate entity*. In the case of a lawsuit, the attorney for the injured party is likely to argue that the corporate entity should not be respected and that the shareholders should be held personally liable. A successful argument here means that the personal assets of the shareholders can be seized to satisfy a judgment. Obviously, from the perspective of asset protection planning, that would be a disaster.

The most obvious circumstance where a court will pierce the corporate veil is when a corporation or entity is used to perpetrate a fraud or a criminal act. Likewise, failing to file tax returns or pay any of the various taxes due will usually result in personal liabilities for the owners of the corporation. Setting those situations aside, the most common reason courts agree to pierce the corporate veil is because the shareholders of a corporation disregard the legal separateness of the corporate form or fail to comply with the formalities required to maintain the corporation.

Many people are lulled into a false sense of security, thinking that once they set up the corporation or other entity, they have no personal liability. Not so. As we saw earlier in this chapter, the act of incorporating is simply one step of many that are required to create and maintain the integrity of the corporate entity. The liability-limiting features of the corporate entity are only available if the corporate requirements are fulfilled. A corporation that fails to adhere to corporate formalities is just a cardboard corporation and can be set aside. Do courts take this formality stuff seriously? You bet they do. According to the *Cornell Law Review*, "95% of corporate veils are pierced when courts determined that shareholders have disregarded the legal separateness of the corporation (or LLC) and the corporation acts as nothing more than an alter ego for the shareholders' own dealings."

When a lawsuit is filed against an asset protection entity, the plaintiff's attorney will secondarily name the individual owners of the entity as defendants and attempt to convince the court that the corporate veil should be pierced and the individual owners held liable. How successful that argument is depends upon how well the entity was formed and maintained.

Some of the factors the court will take into consideration when deciding whether to set aside the corporate entity include the following:

- Was the corporation properly formed, and are corporate records available?
- Was a formal organizational meeting held?
- Were corporate bylaws adopted, and are those bylaws currently being followed?
- Are the officers actually involved with running the corporation?
- Do the shareholders and directors actually have annual meetings, and are there records of those meetings? Even if there's only one shareholder, the court will want to see the meeting formality observed.
- Is there any comingling of funds or assets between shareholders and the corporation?
- Does the corporation maintain separate bank account records and financial books?
- Is the corporation in good standing, and has it filed the annual reports required by the state of incorporation?
- Are the contracts and agreements of the corporation in the corporation's name?
- Was the corporation properly capitalized? In most cases, the transfer of real estate into the corporation would satisfy this requirement.
- Was reasonably adequate insurance maintained on the assets of the corporation?

In addition, the court may consider any other evidence that would indicate that shareholders of the corporation conformed to the requirements of keeping the corporation a separate and distinct entity. The court's reasoning is that if you don't respect the corporate entity, why should it? On the other hand, the courts steadfastly defend the liability protections provided by a properly formed and maintained corporation. The key: the corporation must be "properly formed and maintained."

The legal concept of piercing the corporate veil is not unique to corporations. Other entities are subject to similar attacks and similar scrutiny. In any situation where you create an entity to shield you from liability, be sure you understand the legal requirements of properly maintaining and supporting the integrity of that entity.

Corporations Offer Little Protection from Outside Liabilities

Back in Chapter 2, we learned that there's a difference between inside liabilities and outside liabilities. We used the example of Alice, Bill, and Charlie owning an apartment building in a properly formed limited liability company named Main Street Apartments LLC. Then we looked at what would happen if Bill individually owned and operated a construction business as a sole proprietor and that business failed, resulting in a lawsuit and a judgment against him of $1 million. That judgment, as it relates to the Main Street Apartments LLC, would be considered an outside liability. We saw that Bill's judgment creditor could not seize the apartment building and sell it to satisfy the judgment. Instead the judgment creditor was limited to a "charging order," which only entitled the creditor to receive distributions from the LLC if and when they were made. That same situation might have a completely different outcome if the entity in the example had been a corporation instead of an LLC.

The owners of a corporation are its shareholders, or stockholders. The stock of a corporation is considered the personal property of its individual owner and is subject to being seized to satisfy judgments. So in our example, if Bill's judgment creditor seized Bill's stock in the corporation, the creditor would be able to affect the management through voting proportionate to the stock seized. If Bill owned a majority of the stock, then once that stock was seized, the creditor could actually control the management, vote himself in as director, and then dissolve the corporation, thereby getting access to a proportionate amount of the assets. Because corporations offer no outside liability protection, they are not recommended for long-term real estate investments. Corporations still offer some unique advantages for development projects and subdivisions, but they should not be used for holding or operating apartments or other income property.

Corporation FAQs

What are the different types of corporations?

There are chapter C corporations, subchapter S corporations, professional corporations, mutual benefit corporations, and nonprofit corporations. There are also close corporations and public corporations.

What's the difference between a C corporation and an S corporation?

The difference is in how they are taxed. S corporations elect to be taxed as a pass-through entity (as if the owners were sole proprietors or partners). All corporate profits are reported by the owners as personal income. This type of structure blends the tax advantages of a sole proprietorship or partnership with the limited liability of a corporation. The Internal Revenue Code defines a C corporation as "a corporation which is not an S corporation." This means that its profits are taxed at the corporate level, and then dividends paid to the shareholders are taxed again at the shareholder level.

What's the difference between a close corporation and a public corporation?

A close corporation is owned by a small number of people. A close corporation is also known as a *private corporation* or a *closely held corporation*. The shareholders may or may not participate in the management of the corporation. A public corporation on the other hand, is owned by the general public and has stock listed on one of the stock exchanges. Public corporations have to adhere to significant Securities Exchange Commission regulations.

What are the differences among officers, directors, and shareholders?

A corporation consists of all three: officers, directors, and shareholders. Shareholders are the owners of the corporation and elect the directors. Directors manage the corporation by making all long-term planning decisions. Officers are selected by the directors and run the day-to-day operations of the corporation. In most cases, these roles do not need to be filled by separate people.

Can a single person form a corporation?

Yes, most states allow a single person to be the one required director for a corporation. Likewise, one person can fill all three corporate positions. In small businesses, one individual person can be the lone director, officer, and the only shareholder.

Who manages a corporation?

A corporation is owned by its shareholders. The shareholders elect directors who manage the corporation by appointing officers to handle the day-to-day activities. An appointed officer has the authority to conduct banking activities and deal with tax matters. Generally, a corporation needs to have a president, a treasurer, and a secretary.

What does a corporation's president do?

The president is the chief executive officer (CEO) of the corporation and is usually responsible for the day-to-day operations of the corporation. The president reports to the board of directors. In most cases, the president signs contracts and makes agreements on behalf of the corporation.

What does a corporation's treasurer do?

The treasurer is the chief financial officer (CFO) of the corporation and is usually responsible for the banking activities of the corporation and for keeping accurate and current financial records.

What does a corporation's secretary do?

The secretary is an executive officer of the corporation and is responsible for maintaining records of the corporation, such as minutes of meetings, shareholders lists, etc.

What is an agent for service of process?

Most states require that corporations maintain a designated person (a resident of the state of incorporation) or an entity to be responsible for receiving vital legal and tax documents on behalf of the corporation. That person or entity is usually called an *agent for service of process* or *registered agent*.

What is the registered office?

Some people choose to incorporate in states other than the one in which they live. In those situations, a registered office is usually just the physical street address of your registered agent in that state.

Does a corporation need a registered agent?

Yes. All corporations need a registered agent with a physical street address within the state of formation. This designates a location for legal documents or tax documents to be delivered to the real person who represents the corporation in that capacity. Your attorney would normally act as the initial agent for service of process.

Can a corporation be its own registered agent?

No. A corporation is a legal entity, but all states require that a natural (real) person or state registered corporation be designated the contact for legal and tax matters. However, a shareholder, director, or officer of the corporation can be listed as the agent for service of process.

What is an incorporator?

The incorporator is the person or persons who organize the corporation and file the articles of incorporation. The incorporator is usually your attorney but could also be one of the owners or directors. Once the filing is complete, the person who files the articles of incorporation resigns as the incorporator, thus turning control of the newly formed corporation over to the initial director or directors. This is usually done during the initial organizational meeting.

What is an organizational meeting?

Once you receive the filed articles of incorporation, which signifies the formation of the corporation by your state, your corporation needs to hold an organizational meeting of the initial shareholders and directors. At this meeting, the directors will typically adopt corporate bylaws, issue stock to initial shareholders, and appoint corporate officers.

What are corporate bylaws?

A corporation is required to have bylaws. The bylaws of the corporation describe the internal rules governing the management of the corporation. Bylaws are an internal document of the corporation and are not filed with the state.

Is a corporation required to have ongoing annual meetings?

Yes. Most states require directors to meet at least once a year, because directors must be elected or reelected each year. At the annual meeting, the board members accept their election to the board and transact any other necessary business. The date, time, and location of the annual meeting is typically specified in the bylaws. Even in corporations where only one person is the sole shareholder, sole director, and sole officer, annual meetings are still required.

How many shares of stock will a new corporation need?

The number of initial shares a corporation is authorized to distribute is specified in the articles of incorporation. The amount authorized can be any number—1,500 or 15 million. However, it is important to know the rules of your state, because state fees may be assessed based on how many shares are issued.

What are authorized stock shares?

Authorized shares are the total number of shares that the corporation may distribute or issue. There is no requirement that all authorized shares be issued. Authorized but unissued shares are not included in any calculation of corporate or shareholder equity.

What are issued stock shares?

Issued shares are the authorized shares that have actually been issued or sold to shareholders. The number of authorized shares is not always the same as the numbers of issued shares. Unissued shares do not represent an equity holding in the corporation. A shareholder's equity is determined based on the total number of shares actually issued.

What is stock par value?

Par value is an arbitrary dollar amount given to corporate shares. It doesn't necessarily reflect their real value and is typically set at one dollar. The par value of a share is the minimum price at which it may be sold to shareholders, and the par value must be the same for all shares of the same class.

How are stock shares issued?

Stock certificates are created and "sold" to the initial shareholders at the initial organizational meeting. Some degree of formality is required, so usually your attorney would perform this task for you. The issued stock certificates represent the ownership of the corporation, so it's important that stock be issued correctly.

6 Limited Liability Companies (LLCs)

IN THE PAST 20 years, limited liability companies (LLCs) have grown dramatically in popularity. The LLC is best viewed as a hybrid combination of a partnership and a corporation, merging many of the advantages of each and eliminating many of the disadvantages of both. Many people mistakenly referred to LLCs as "LLPs" (which actually stands for "limited liability *partnerships*") or as "limited liability *corporations*." LLCs are neither partnerships nor corporations. Like corporations, LLCs have strong liability-limiting characteristics; however, they do not have the rigorous formal requirements of having corporate directors, officers, and annual meetings. Instead, the LLC is run by a designated managing member or collectively by all members and is controlled by an operating agreement created at the time of formation. Then, like partnerships, LLCs have a simplified pass-through tax treatment and offer entity asset protection from outside (individual member) liabilities. In most cases, LLCs are the best entity choice for holding long-term real estate investments like apartment buildings and other rental property.

Have LLCs Replaced the Corporation?

There has been a lot of talk lately suggesting that the limited liability company (LLC) has replaced the subchapter S corporation. Given that both entities are very similar but the LLC seems to be less formal and, therefore, less burdensome, common sense suggests that the simpler entity would replace the original. Upon further review, it becomes apparent that these two entities serve similar purposes for different types of ventures.

Both the LLC and the S corporation provide a pass-through entity for taxation purposes and limited liability for the shareholders (in the case of the subchapter S corporation) and the members (in the case of the LLC). However, how they provide those benefits is different, making each suitable for differing ventures. For example, when deciding between the S corporation and the LLC for long-term real estate investment purposes (holding for appreciation and/or rental income), the majority of real estate investors would go with the LLC structure. On the other hand, you may be interested in doing a subdivision or a short-term fix-and-flip property. In this case, the S corporation offers some advantages that the LLC does not. The reason the two entities are suitable for different investments comes back to our dealer-versus-investor discussion. The former venture looks more like an investor's business, whereas the latter looks more like a dealer's.

Dealers have ongoing business concerns with their properties, and the S corporation offers advantages in the way that taxes can be structured. For example, in a normal ongoing business entity, the shareholder of the corporation may choose to take a salary as an employee of the corporation from a portion of the profits that are generated from the activity of the entity. From there, the shareholder would take the remaining profits as a distribution. Why would you want to do that? In the case of an ongoing business concern, the earnings of the business (whether in a sole proprietorship, a partnership, or an LLC) are passed through to the owner of the business and are considered self-employment income. Self-employment income incurs self-employment taxes as well as some other federal taxes associated with it. That same profit being distributed to a subchapter S corporation shareholder is not earmarked as self-employment income and, therefore, avoids those taxes on an ongoing basis. This makes the S corporation a better choice for the property dealer.

On the other hand, a property investor does not have ongoing income from the venture and will not need an entity with the formalities of a corporation, so an LLC is better suited for him. The S corporation still has some very valuable uses, so the LLC is not going to replace the S corporation. Instead, these two entities will exist alongside each other, offering similar asset protection and pass-through taxation, just for different ventures.

Most real estate investors who will read this book are exactly that: investors. As such, the vast majority of the readers would probably opt for the LLC structure. There are some other differences in regards to allowable write-offs for the different entities, but these concerns come after the initial consideration of dealer versus investor, and the majority of readers will still go with the LLC. With that said, we will now focus on the facets of the LLC.

Tax Differences and Considerations

As stated earlier, an LLC can be taxed as a pass-through entity. What does that mean? A pass-through entity means that the entity structure exists but does not pay taxes itself; rather, the entity files a tax return and issues what's called a K-1. Each K-1 goes out to the members of the LLC, and the responsibility for paying taxes, taking losses, etc. is passed through to the members; hence, the name *pass-through entity*.

There are many advantages to pass-through taxation. The first and most obvious is that the entity itself does not pay taxes. Unlike a C corporation, which is required to pay its own taxes and pass the net profits to the shareholders, who must then pay income taxes on the distributions, an LLC does not suffer from this double-taxation scheme. The pass-through taxation makes the LLC more advantageous than a standard C corporation. Second, LLC members have the ability to take losses on the LLC, while corporation shareholders cannot. Additionally, some expenses can be written off by an LLC that otherwise could not. An LLC has the asset protection shell of a corporation but the pass-through taxation advantages of a partnership.

The single-member LLC must be considered separately. Single-member LLCs are usually entities that are owned by one person, although in some states, an LLC owned by a married couple can be considered a single-member LLC. This entity is basically a disregarded entity for tax-filing purposes. Because of this, the sole owner of the single-member LLC reports all of the profits, deductions, credits allowed to the business, etc. on a schedule C, which is filed with her individual tax return (just as a sole proprietor would do). There is no separate corporate return to file. This is in contrast to the multimember LLC, which must file an entity tax return, although it does not pay taxes with that return. In some situations, the single-member is the simplest form of tax filing while still offering some level of limited liability and asset protection at the entity level.

The members of a multimember LLC may elect to be taxed as a corporation. There would not be much reason to do this unless there was some bigger, grander plan for the LLC. For our purposes in this book dealing with basic real estate investment, this approach would not make sense.

Formalities of Formation

The Articles of Organization

An LLC is created by the filing of articles of organization. Much like a corporation's articles of incorporation, articles of organization are filed with the state in which the LLC will operate. It is possible to organize an LLC in a state other than where the LLC will be operating. In most situations, however, you file the articles of organization in the state in which you intend to do business. In this book, we're referring to real estate investment, so you might file the LLC where a real estate investment is located. The LLC is not limited to holding property in that state. For example, you might have an Arizona LLC that owns an apartment building in Arizona. At some point, the LLC may sell that property, do a 1031 exchange, and purchase another property in another state. The Arizona LLC, now the owner of the newly acquired property in a different state, would simply need to file the proper paperwork (register) to do business in that state. Likewise, that Arizona LLC could concurrently own multiple properties in multiple states. Again, most of the time, you would file your articles of organization in the state where you're located or in the state where the real estate investment is located, but you are not limited to doing so.

Filing the articles of organization is a pretty basic procedure. Most states' departments of corporations or departments of business (whatever it may be in your state) have some procedure for filing the articles of organization. Often, the state even provides a form that you use to file the articles of organization. Again, filing your articles of organization with the state to tell it that you will be doing business as a limited liability company is just the first step of many that must be accomplished for your LLC to be solid and actually provide the desired limited liability and asset protection.

The Operating Agreement

Many people don't give the operating agreement the attention that it deserves. The operating agreement of a limited liability company is very similar to the bylaws of a corporation in that it lays out and documents the structure of the organization. It establishes the formal structure of the entity and includes information like whether the LLC is managed by managers or managed by members (remember that the term *members* refers to the owners in an LLC). It says how many managers there will be and how many members there will be. It documents the liabilities of the members, as well as whether the members will make contributions to the LLC. Additionally, it identifies the positions of persons who have certain responsibilities. This is especially important down the line, because these designations are required for transferring property, conducting banking activities, insuring property, and signing contracts on behalf of the LLC. The operating agreement, on the whole, lays out the structure of how things are to be operated within the entity shell. The operating agreement is what banks, title insurance companies, liability insurance companies, and mortgage lenders need to see to establish the structure of your LLC and know who is authorized to do business on behalf of the entity. Without a properly drafted operating agreement, you will not be able to conduct normal business affairs as an LLC. Likewise, as we'll see in an upcoming section, the failure to have a valid operating agreement is strong evidence supporting an argument that the members of the LLC should be held personally liable for the debts of the LLC.

Minutes and Appointing the LLC "Manager(s)"

Next you must consider the organizational meeting. The minutes document the decisions made in the organizational meeting of an LLC, just as the minutes document the decisions made in the organizational meeting of a corporation. There is a difference, though. Because of its less rigid formality, the LLC does not require an annual meeting, and, thus, there are no annual minutes. Therefore, the minutes of the first organizational meeting simply document the fact that the operating agreement was adopted and that the meeting took place. Unlike the corporation, which has a set of bylaws that lays down the structure and has the minutes to fill the structure, the LLC operating agreement can set down the structure *and* fill it. So many times, naming managers can be done right in the operating agreement. If future changes are made, such as naming different managers, you'll make an amendment to the operating agreement or adopt a revised operating agreement. However, you can still use minutes to document your changes, if you prefer. Whether you maintain minutes or draft amendments to your operating agreement is up to you. Generally speaking, more businesslike documentation is better than less.

Regardless of whether you are going to maintain minutes or try to draft your operating agreement at the organizational meeting, some of the things that need to take place during the organizational meeting include appointing managers, designating who will be responsible for banking activities, and identifying the main place of business, to name a few.

How Ownership Interests Are Defined and Issued

In the operating agreement, you establish how many members (owners) the LLC will have. The minutes then spell out who those members are and what their contributions will be. The minutes would state specifically that, for example, George has contributed $2,000 and he owns 10 percent of the LLC. Because members' contributions can change yearly, they are dictated in the minutes instead of written into the operating agreement. In the case of a single-member LLC, obviously we're talking about one member making a contribution of perhaps an apartment building and that same owner owning 100 percent of the LLC. There could be many different variations on that, however, so defining ownership interest goes structurally in the operating agreement, and then the variables are stipulated in the minutes of the meeting.

What You Will Need to Conduct Business and Banking

The minutes of the meeting is also where we sometimes define who has the authority to conduct banking activities. *Banking activities* means quite a bit: who has the ability to open a bank account and who has the ability to sign checks. Both of those things must be delineated in some type of a formal structure so that when the LLC's authorized representative walks into the bank, he has paperwork to show the entity's existence, how it will be operated, and proof that he in fact has the authorization to conduct the banking. Additionally, the LLC will also need a tax ID number just like a corporation. You will need all of those things just to open a bank account and be able to write checks. Figure 6.1 shows an overview of the process of organizing an LLC.

Cost to Create and Operate an LLC

Much of this section on the costs of creating and operating an LLC is similar to the section on the costs of creating and operating a corporation (in Chapter 5). If you read that section already, you may want to glance through this and move on to the next section. However, I know that when I read a book like this, I tend to jump to the chapters that are of interest to me. Because I assume other people like me out there may have skipped ahead to this chapter before reading the corporations chapter, I have included this section again. It is written to pertain to LLCs, but much of the information is the same.

Using an Attorney to Form Your LLC

Using an attorney to form your LLC is advisable. The purpose of creating your LLC in the first place is to provide limited liability and asset protection. The liability protection of any entity will depend upon its structure and integrity. How it was formed, how it is operated, and whether all the rules are being followed properly all influence whether the liability protection of an LLC will actually work when you need it. Unless you're willing to devote a lot of your time to learning this area of law, then it is advisable to have an attorney create your limited liability company.

The expense of having an attorney help you create your LLC is not that much more than that of any of the alternatives that we'll discuss in just a moment. You might spend a few hundred dollars more, but by

FIGURE 6.1 *Flow Chart of the LLC Organization Process*

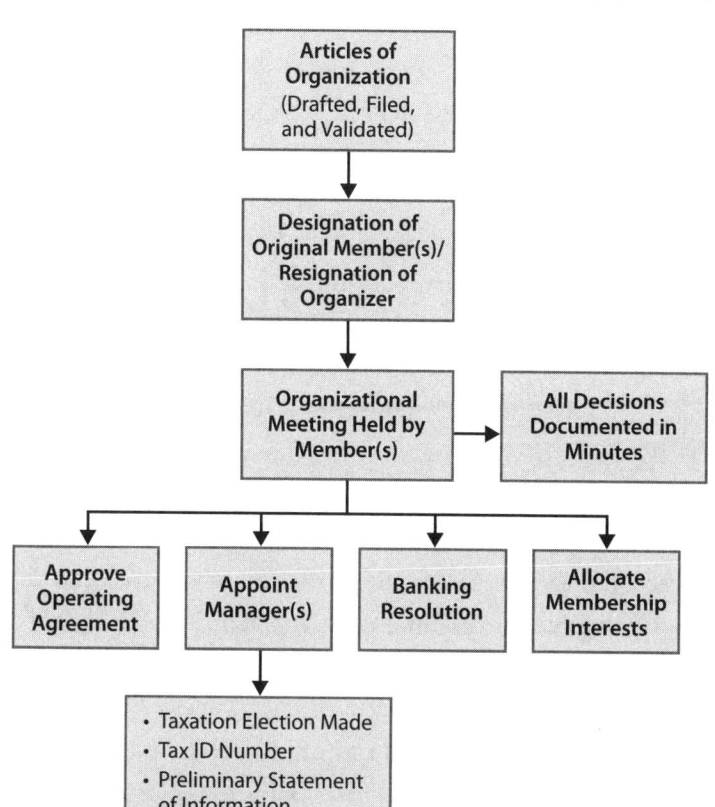

using an attorney, you will sidestep most of the problems others run into and it is the only way you will really know your LLC is solid.

How do you choose an attorney? This area of law (asset protection and entity formation) is a specialization, so you will need to find an attorney who does this every day as part of her legal practice. The best way to find the right attorney is to get a reference from a friend or an associate who has used the attorney in the past. Each attorney sets his own fees for this kind of work. You should be able to get a ballpark estimate of what forming your LLC will cost with a simple phone call to the lawyer's office.

If the staff won't give you a ballpark range, find another attorney. You might look for a recommendation from your accountant or somebody whom you know who has an LLC. Just make sure that the person you know actually used an attorney to draft the LLC. You would not want to take the recommendation of your buddy, Bob, who bought a kit and tells you, "Oh, come on. It's easy!" Bob very likely has a false sense of security about his LLC and won't know if there's anything wrong with it until it's too late. (Go back and read the section titled "Cardboard Corporations" in Chapter 5; the same thing applies to LLCs.)

Another way to find an attorney might be to use a referral service. Your state bar association likely has referral services for different types of attorneys. If you're in Los Angeles or Orange County, California, you can call my office—I'm located in Long Beach, and my contact information can be found in the Appendix.

The cost of having a reasonably priced attorney file an LLC and create the organizational documents (the operating agreement and the minutes of the first meeting) should be somewhere around $1,000. In some cases, that amount will include the filing fees for the state and all the miscellaneous things that need to be completed, and in some cases, it won't. In large metropolitan areas (e.g., Chicago, Los Angeles, or New York), the service might be quite a bit more expensive.

The most important part is being sure that you get good advice and that your LLC is properly formed. Having said that, there are a lot of other ways to get an LLC formed. One is through online companies.

Online LLC Formation Services

First and foremost, the purpose of an online LLC service is presumably to save money. We assume this because online services don't offer advice, they don't guarantee their service, they don't provide the level of formalities that are necessary to validate an LLC, and all of their disclaimers will tell you that you are basically on your own. Why else would you settle for so little service unless you were trying to save money? If you really want to save that couple hundred dollars, just be aware that you will have to complete much of the work to create your LLC properly and steer clear of trouble yourself. The online services will not perform certain tasks for you for any amount of money. They are not allowed to practice law, and if you look at the disclaimer after any one of their sales pitches, you will see that what they do is very limited and you are agreeing that you are either knowledgeable in this area or that you will be seeking the advice of an attorney. They also stress that they are not providing you any legal service or guidance of that nature. Some snippets of online company disclaimers follow:

> Our services not intended to replace the advice of an attorney. . . . All services are provided as-is with no representations or warranties. . . . You assume complete responsibility and risk for use of this site and any/all site-related services. . . . By using this service, you waive any rights or claims you may have. . . . We are not a law firm, and our employees are not acting as your attorney; instead, you are representing yourself and are solely responsible. . . . This Web site is not a substitute for the advice of an attorney. . . . You should consult a licensed attorney in your area. . . . The information provided by this Web site is not guaranteed to be correct, complete, or up-to-date. . . . You agree that you have been advised of the possibility of loss or damage and hereby waive any and all claims. . . .

Figure 6.2 shows the steps of the LLC organization process that the online companies actually provide. I've had to fix way too many botched LLC filings for me to recommend that anyone use online services for something this important. Nonetheless, we must take a look at what they offer.

What exactly do these services do for you? The advertised rate is usually for filing the article of organization—nothing else. If you've formed

FIGURE 6.2 *Online Companies' Services*

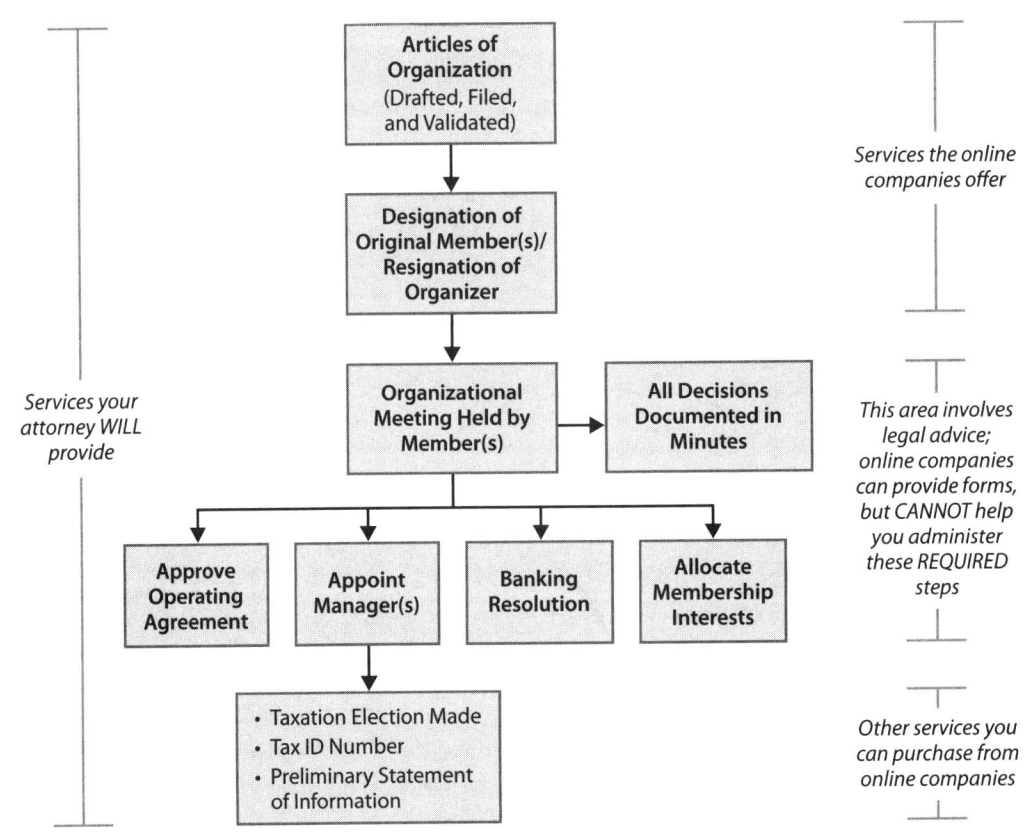

eight or nine LLCs yourself and you are very familiar with entity formation, you probably would be able to use one of these services because you will know what you still need to do when their service ends. Unless you have that experience, you're going to get a false sense of security that your online service took care of what you needed. In reality, all these services do is file an articles of organization document with the state and hand you a bunch of fill-in-the-blank documents. Those fill-in-the-blank documents are the same ones they use for Florida, South Dakota, Ohio, California, or any other state. To these services, it doesn't matter that each one of those states has different laws and different LLC requirements. It doesn't matter to the people who use these services either, until they get sued. So for a couple hundred dollars, you can buy a generic LLC package that probably won't help you under the laws of your state. Why bother?

We have already established that using an online service is presumably to save money. Does this approach actually save money, though? These services' advertising tells you that forming your LLC costs $150 (or whatever amount). In reality, that is just the charge for filing the one-page articles of organization with the state. Frankly, if that's all you need to do, you can get that form from the state and mail it off for only the cost of a postage stamp. As you look further, you will see that they likely want you to buy some LLC kit that costs more money. Then if you want the job done within two or three weeks, they will charge you extra for what is supposedly "rush service." If you want the premium package, it's another $600; if you want a tax ID number, it will cost $70; your statement of information is $100 . . . and this is $5 and that is $10. It just keeps going on and on. As you check the boxes and move through the order process at one of these online registration forms, you should start to realize the service will cost you as much as using any real attorney would—and you're still not getting any legal advice! Table 6.1 gives you a comparison of prices and services between a leading online company and an attorney. You can see that you would pay almost as much for the online service—and still sign the disclaimer that says you realize you are not receiving any guidance whatsoever and that you are basically on your own. Again, why bother?

Some of the online sites actually look professional and pretty convincing. But who are these people? There are hundreds of them. No license is required to operate one of these online companies. No experience or education is needed. No one checks their credentials or their backgrounds. For all anybody knows, the whole business exists on the laptop computer of some college student. In fact, a lot of online sites are

TABLE 6.1 *Comparison of Online Service and Attorney's Service*

	Leading Online Company Basic Package ($150)	Leading Online Company Premium Package ($770)	Attorney ($1,000)
Preliminary Name Search	✓	✓	✓
Preparation and Filing Articles of Organization	✓	✓	✓
Operating Agreement Form	✓	✓	✓
Operating Agreement Completed and Validated	Not Provided	Not Provided	✓
Resolutions Drafted	Not Provided	Not Provided	✓
Membership Interest Certificates	Not Provided	Not Provided	✓
Membership Interest Issued	Not Provided	Not Provided	✓
LLC Kit (includes binder and seal)	$100	✓	✓
Minutes Form	✓	✓	✓
Minutes Completed and Validated	Not Provided	Not Provided	✓
Tax ID Number	$70	✓	✓
Statement of Information	$100	✓	✓
Conduct Organizational Meeting*	Not Provided	Not Provided	✓
Deeding Property**	Not Provided	Not Provided	✓
Five to Ten Business Day Service	$165	$165	✓
Legal Advice on All Steps of the Process, Taking into Account Individual Nuances	Not Provided	Not Provided	✓
All Forms Completed for You, with No Time Spent Figuring Out the Process	Not Provided	Not Provided	✓
Registered Agent for First Year	$160	✓	✓
Shipping and Handling for Your Documents	$20	$20	✓
Person with Legal Responsibility for Errors***	YOU	YOU	ATTORNEY
Actual Cost (not including state filing fees)	$765	$955	$1,000

* Required for proper formation but not provided AT ALL by online services.
** Has SERIOUS tax implications but not provided AT ALL by online services.
*** This item alone could be worth thousands of dollars and should negate any difference in start-up costs.

Notice that certain items are REQUIRED but not offered at all by the online company. You will either have to figure them out yourself or hire an attorney anyway. By using an attorney, not only do you get these additional items but you get peace of mind; with the online companies, you get, at best, a false sense of security.

run by high school or college kids. They know the Internet, they know how to design Web pages, and they know they never have to meet you face-to-face. All they really need is to copy some generic forms from other sites and get a fax program to send articles of organization to the different states, and viola, they are in business! As amazing as it sounds, it's entirely possible that the online company who's creating those LLCs knows less about it than you do. Is that really who you want creating your asset protection entities?

Do-It-Yourself Books, Kits, and Software

Do-it-yourself books, kits, and software are just like online services in that they are designed to save you a little money. At least with the do-it-yourself books and kits, you're forced to learn how to do it right. If you have a lot of time on your hands and you're willing to commit that time to learning this area of law, maybe the do-it-yourself books or kits are right for you. Still, don't forget that forming the LLC is just one of many steps that need to be taken.

Real Estate Deeding Process and Mortgage Pitfalls

Because this book is primarily for real estate investors, we need to look at the details of transferring property into whatever asset protection entity is created. I had a client once with a favorite saying: "You don't know what you don't know until you know it." By that, he meant that you won't know that you did something wrong until there's a problem, and then, of course, it's too late because it's already done. That's especially true when preparing deeds for real estate transfers. It seems as though you could simply copy the last deed and change some of the words around, and that's all there is to it. Right? Wrong. Real estate transfers are part of a very complex area of law. Even actions as simple as transferring property into or out of an entity can cause all kinds of problems, problems you won't even know exist for years.

Real estate transfers are another reason you should hire a competent attorney. Online services, books, kits, and software are not going to help. In this area, there is no substitute for experience, and mistakes are very costly.

In each state, there is a proper way to draft a deed; messing it up can cause all kinds of problems. As an attorney, I have seen situations where people have tried to save a little bit of money, and thinking that drafting a deed would be easy, they did it themselves. When they're done, it's usually a mess; they usually *create a cloud on the title* (meaning that the title is unclear) or some other problem. In one case, a client drafted a deed intending to add someone to the title so that my client and this other person were jointly on title (they were newly entering partners). When my client was done, what he had actually accomplished (and recorded) was a deed that conveyed the entire property to the other person. He no longer owned any interest in the property!

It seems as though making that kind of mistake would be difficult, but real estate deeds contain complex and archaic language and errors are common. The language involved in a deed is very specific, and if written incorrectly, a number of things can happen: a cloud on the title could appear, a conveyance could be made incorrectly, income taxes could be triggered, or reassessment of property taxes could be triggered. Additionally, incorrectly deeding a property could create a situation where the property is never actually transferred into the entity. If the entity never owns it, the entity can't protect you from the liability of that property or offer asset protection for the property. All of these things are in the realm of lawyers, and without having an extensive background in it, a person should be smart enough to protect any investment by having the deeding done properly.

Transferring property into an LLC or any other entity also raises mortgage, property insurance, and title insurance issues that need to be addressed. Just about every mortgage on the property has what's called a *due-on-sale clause* or *due-on-transfer clause*. That means the mortgage holder wants to be paid off if the property is sold or transferred. See the problem? If you transfer an apartment building into an LLC, you are probably in violation of your due-on-transfer clause. That means the lender can *call the note*, requiring you to pay it off or refinance the property. Obviously, that can be disastrous if current interest rates are higher than your existing mortgage rates.

The same kind of contractual issue comes up regarding your liability insurance on the property. Your landlord policy probably names you as the insured. If you transfer the building into an LLC, you no longer own the insured building, and the insurance company doesn't have a policy issued to the LLC. If it's left like that and you have to make a significant claim on the insurance, you might find your insurance company is no longer your friend. Likewise, title insurance on the property was issued to the person who bought it. Once the property is transferred to the LLC, the title insurance company will give you some resistance if you make a claim without first notifying it and getting its approval of the transfer.

All of these potential problems are avoidable if you know what to do. But remember: "You don't know what you don't know, until you know it." These kinds of issues are exactly why people hire an attorney instead of trying to go it alone.

Agent for Service of Process Choices

Like corporations, every LLC is required to designate a registered agent or agent for service of process. If you are the sole owner of your LLC, the most obvious choice for the agent for service of process might be you. This is certainly an option; the owner of an LLC is allowed to be its agent for service of process. Still, you might want to consider some factors before making that choice.

The first consideration is privacy. If you have created an LLC to own real estate or to house a real estate venture or investment, you can name the LLC anything you like. It does not need to have your name on it at all. If you'd prefer that people not know who you are or who owns the actual venture or investment, you might name your entity Main Street Properties LLC. That alone would not give anybody any indication of who owns it; additionally, looking it up on the property tax records would just simply show that an LLC is the owner of the property or venture. The next step for someone interested in finding the owner would be to go to the state's department of corporations Web site, which likely has a public database providing various information on the LLCs registered in that state. Typing in the name of the LLC, you could get the name of the registered agent or agent for service of process. If privacy is important to you, you don't want your name and address posted here. Let's take a look at an example:

> Harry Doe owns an apartment building and places that apartment building in an LLC named Main Street Properties LLC. He has significant other assets and wants to make sure that no lawsuits from the LLC property create a risk for his other assets. Unfortunately, Harry Doe names himself as the agent for service of process. Also, Harry doesn't have an office, so he lists his home address as the mailing address for the agent for service of process.
>
> Anybody who looks up the tax records for the LLC property will get the name Main Street Properties LLC. Then a quick check of the state department of corporations database would display that the named agent for service of process is Harry Doe along with his home address. It doesn't take a genius to figure out that Harry Doe owns the property (or is at least one of the owners). Now anybody could have Harry Doe's name, home address, and the ability to quickly search for Harry's other assets.

Many of my clients don't like the idea of having their names and addresses so easily accessible, so whom they name as agent for service of process becomes an important consideration.

Once you have decided that you don't want your name listed as the agent for service of process, your next step is to decide who that agent will be. Professional and online companies offer this service for a set fee per year. It is probably well worth spending the money to maintain your privacy. The caution here is that you need to be careful whom you hire to provide that service.

When an attorney is first considering whether filing a lawsuit against your LLC will be worthwhile, one of the things she will look at is how well you followed the LLC formalities. In other words, did you do everything properly so that your entity will actually bar a plaintiff from coming after your personal assets? The first clue the attorney will have in this regard is who is listed as your agent for service of process. If you and your home address are listed or if you have listed some dot-com as the agent, the assumption is that you are not being advised by a lawyer. That suggests a higher probability that in a lawsuit, your LLC will not be able to protect your personal assets. On the other hand, if your listed agent is a licensed attorney, it sends a whole different message. Now the presumption is that your attorney will be able to make that LLC do what it was intended to do: protect your personal assets from attack.

Dealing with Government Agencies

Every time you file or create an entity, you essentially put yourself on the radar of a number of different government agencies, all of which have something to do with taxes or other business regulations. If you don't create your entity properly, you will hear from the state employment department, the state tax board, the IRS, the state department of corporations, and perhaps many others. If you use an attorney to set up your LLC, then most of the time, you will just forward these things to your attorney. He will either take care of it or let you know what you need to do to take care of it; in many cases, you don't need to do anything. For many of my clients, I take care of all that correspondence, because it can be mind-boggling unless you're used to it.

Regardless of what agency the correspondence comes from or who helps you discern what the agency wants, you must not ignore it. It is important that you respond to correspondence appropriately and in a timely fashion so that something simple doesn't suddenly turn into threats, penalties, and "noncompliance." Not knowing or understanding what the agency wants from you does not excuse you from the penalties resulting from nonresponsiveness.

Moreover, incorrectly responding or not responding at all to an agency's request is an indication that your entity is not a sound structure. Remember, you want to be structurally solid—and appear structurally solid.

Using Service Companies

Because so many formalities, so much mail, and so many other things come with forming an entity, companies have surfaced to help you take care of these things. They will, for a set fee, take care of the ongoing formalities and field all the questions that come up in response to mail and interaction with the many different government agencies. Many of those service companies are comprised of attorneys in firms that either work together or independently as advisors to entities. For some people, using such a company is a good idea. Again, you want to make sure that what you create will serve the purpose for which it is created, and if you do not know how to do these things, then you're at risk.

Piercing the LLC Veil

In the chapter on corporations, we looked at the legal doctrine known as "piercing the corporate veil." More and more courts are applying similar standards to LLCs, and a new piercing-the–LLC-veil doctrine is evolving. A handful of states have even codified application of the piercing-the-veil doctrine to LLCs. In California for example, Corporations Code §17101(b) reads (emphasis added):

> A member of a limited liability company shall be subject to liability under the common law governing alter ego liability, and shall also be *personally liable* under a judgment of a court or for any debt, obligation, or liability of the limited liability company, whether that liability or obligation arises in contract, tort, or otherwise, under the same or similar circumstances and *to the same extent as a shareholder of a corporation may be personally liable* for any debt, obligation, or liability of the corporation; *except that the failure to hold meetings of members or managers or the failure to observe formalities pertaining to the calling or conduct of meetings shall not be considered* a factor tending to establish that a member or the members have alter ego or personal liability for any debt, obligation, or liability of the limited liability company where the articles of organization or operating agreement do not expressly require the holding of meetings of members or managers.

The two points of interest from this code section are that it specifically applies the same common law piercing-the-corporate-veil standards to LLCs and that it then expressly excuses them from having to observe the formalities of calling or holding meetings. In California LLCs, this code is bittersweet at best; it says the formality of meetings is no longer necessary but all other corporation like formalities must be followed.

So when an argument is being made to pierce the LLC veil, courts will ask the following:

- Was the LLC properly formed, and are LLC records available?
- Was a formal organizational meeting held?

- Was an operating agreement created, and is it being followed?
- Is there any comingling of funds or assets between members and the LLC?
- Does the LLC maintain separate bank account records and financial books?
- Is the LLC in good standing and filing the annual reports required by the state of incorporation?
- Are the contracts and agreements of the LLC in the LLC's name?
- Was the LLC properly capitalized?
- Was adequate insurance maintained on the property in the LLC?

The primary reason to create any entity is to limit the liability of the owners and/or to protect assets in the entity. One of the most commonly cited reasons for choosing an LLC over a corporation is the "relaxed" formality requirement. Yet, as you can see from the list above, *relaxed* doesn't really mean "r e l a x e d." Nevertheless, simply getting rid of the annual meeting formality is a significant benefit. So, as with corporations, the most common reason courts agree to pierce the veil is when the members (owners) of the LLC disregard the legal separateness of the entity form or fail to comply with formalities. Annual meetings are out, but other formalities still exist and must be observed.

In addition, any time an entity is used to perpetrate a fraud or commit criminal activity, the LLC entity will be disregarded. Likewise, LLCs created for fraudulent transfer purposes will be set aside as well.

Asset Protection and the Charging Order

Up to this point, we've focused on limiting the liability from inside debts. Back in Chapter 2, we talked about how *inside debts* are those liabilities that arise from the assets in the LLC. In a real estate investment LLC, we are usually talking about lawsuits that occur from something happening on the property. In this section, we're going to focus on outside liabilities and asset protection. By *outside liabilities*, I'm referring to judgments against individual LLC members, unrelated to the LLC.

In the example in Chapter 2, Bill, a member of an LLC, also owned a construction company as a sole proprietor. The construction company failed, and one of the construction company creditors got a judgment for $1 million against Bill. In that example, I said the judgment creditor's remedy would be limited to obtaining a "charging order" against the member's interest. Charging order protection is considered one of the key features an LLC provides that a corporation does not. But what is a charging order?

The LLC statutes in all states are based on the the Uniform Limited Liability Company Act of 1996, Revised Uniform Partnership Act of 1994, or the Uniform Limited Partnership Act of 2001. All three of these Uniform Acts provide the basis for what remedies are available to a creditor pursuing a partnership member's interest in a partnership or LLC. I could spend the next five pages citing these Acts and the evolution of charging orders, but I will spare you the lawyer-speak and get to the bottom line:

- A charging order is the *exclusive* remedy for creditors pursuing a member's interest in an LLC.
- A charging order is similar to a lien or a garnishment on the debtor/member's transferable interest and *only* entitles the creditor to the debtor/member's share of distributions, if any.
- A judgment creditor may foreclose on a charging order (lien), forcing the sale of the debtor/member's transferable interest only, *not* the LLC assets.
- The purchaser at a foreclosure sale of a debtor/member's transferable interest receives *only* the rights of the assignee/transferee.

- A judgment creditor or a purchaser of the debtor/member's can *never* exercise any management, voting rights, or direct distributions from the LLC.

To put this in perspective, let's go back to the earlier example where one member (the "debtor/member") of an LLC is being individually pursued for the $1 million judgment. Let's say the LLC has three equal members and owns one apartment building valued at $3 million. Obviously, a judgment creditor is going to want access to that asset. Applying the points above, however, we first see that the judgment creditor only has one remedy: a charging order. Second, the charging order as a lien only entitles the judgment creditor to distributions if and when the LLC chooses to make them. Third, the judgment creditor could foreclose on the debtor/member's transferable interest and sell it to satisfy the debt. Fourth, anyone who buys that transferable interest only gets the rights of an assignee/transferee (along with some potential tax problems that we will discuss). Fifth, nowhere in this process does a judgment creditor or assignee/transferee get any rights to influence the decisions, management, or distributions of the LLC.

Obviously, if you're a creditor of an LLC debtor member, this charging order remedy and process is not very appealing. The laws created here seem to favor the LLC debtor member, but not necessarily. One of the primary goals in creating the Uniform Acts was to provide stability and certainty in partnership and LLC business dealings. The charging order is intended to strike a balance between the needs of allowing a remedy for judgment creditors while still protecting the rights of the other LLC nondebtor members.

You may be thinking that works well as an asset protection tool for the nondebtor members but not so well for the debtor member, because that person still ends up losing transferable interest in the LLC. But that's not always the case. A cleverly drafted LLC operating agreement can make it very unattractive for a creditor to pursue this remedy at all. Likewise, a judgment creditor who pursues this remedy through foreclosure of the transferable interest becomes responsible for paying taxes on that corresponding portion of the LLC's taxable income. Because an assignee/transferee has no right to affect management decisions or profit distributions, and tax liability is passed through to the members regardless of whether distributions are actually made, it is actually possible for an assignee/transferee to owe taxes on that portion of the LLC profits without ever receiving any money. As a practical matter, the situation rarely occurs, because judgment creditors aren't stupid enough to put themselves in that position. Nevertheless, the potential of this negative tax aspect results in a very limited resale market for foreclosed LLC interests and strongly encourages judgment creditors to settle. The fact is, judgment creditors rarely pursue charging orders in situations like this, and that is the primary asset protection benefit for the debtor/member.

It's very important to understand that the rationale for making the charging order the judgment creditor's exclusive remedy is to protect the interests of the nondebtor members. That being said, arguably, if the LLC has only one member (a single-member LLC), there are no nondebtor members to protect so charging order restrictions should not apply. There are a few cases on the books in which a court allowed the judgment creditor to seize the assets in a single-member LLC situation. As such, special attention should be given to this aspect in deciding whether to form a single-member LLC.

In summary, LLCs appear to be an outstanding entity form for real estate investors. The fact that LLCs offer the same liability-limiting features of a corporation and provide excellent asset protection from outside liabilities makes them very attractive. Add to that the ease of formation, relaxed ongoing formalities, and pass-through tax treatment and you can quickly see why LLCs are becoming the entity of choice.

Real Estate Investor LLC FAQs

What are the different LLCs used by real estate investors?

Traditional LLCs are broken down into two categories: single-member and multimember. LLCs owned by one individual or a husband and wife are considered single-member LLCs. Multimember LLCs have more than one person and can either be member managed or manager managed. Both structures are appropriate for holding real estate investments. There's also a new entity called a series LLC (see Chapter 7) and the family limited liability company, or FLLC.

Can one person form an LLC?

Yes, in most states. However, it is important to note that some of the asset protection features designed to protect LLC assets from outside liability can be challenged and possibly set aside in single-member LLCs.

Which is better for real estate investments: LLCs or S corporations?

S corporations are better for ongoing active businesses, and LLCs are better for long-term real estate investments. Both offer pass-through tax treatment, and both offer limited liability from debts arising from within the entity. LLCs are generally preferred for their relaxed formality requirements. LLCs also offer superior asset protection from outside liabilities.

How is an LLC formed?

Each state requires the filing of an organizational document called the "articles of organization" or some similar name. Some states have additional preformation requirements. Once the articles of organization have been filed, the members (owners) create an operating agreement, which gives structure to the organization and names those persons who are authorized to act on behalf of the LLC.

Does an LLC have to file tax returns?

Yes and no. Single-member LLCs are disregarded entities for tax purposes. The single-member LLC owner would report income and losses on a Schedule C of his personal tax return. Multimember LLCs are treated like a partnership for tax-reporting purposes. The tax return is filed for the entity, K-1 forms are issued to the LLC members, and the profits are recognized and taxed on personal tax returns.

Does an LLC have to hold annual meetings?

No. One of the advantages of the LLC entity over an S corporation is a relaxed degree of formality. Annual state filings still need to be completed as well as other requirements, but overall, LLCs require much less ongoing administration.

Does an LLC have stock?

No. LLCs have membership certificates. LLC membership certificates are issued in much the same way as corporation stock. Likewise, LLC membership certificates have a similar "look and feel" as corporation stock certificates.

Who issues the LLC membership certificates?

LLC membership certificates are usually prepared by your attorney and issued in the initial organizational meeting. At that meeting, an operating agreement would be agreed upon by the members, and membership certificates would be issued at that time.

Why does an LLC have to have articles of organization and an operating agreement?

Articles of organization are filed with the state and merely show the existence of the LLC. The operating agreement gives structure to the organization, sets out who its members (owners) are, and provides documentation showing who is authorized to act on behalf of the LLC. Both the articles of organization and a valid operating agreement will be required to conduct most business activities on behalf of the LLC.

How do you transfer investment property to an LLC?

Usually transfers are done by grant deed or a similar conveyance instrument. Many potential problems are association with conveying property to an LLC. Seeking the appropriate legal advice is always recommended.

Can LLCs do 1031 exchanges?

Yes. LLC-owned investment property qualifies for 1031 tax-deferred exchange treatment. Note, however, that a 1031 exchange commenced in an LLC must be completed in that same LLC.

Can I take an investment property back out of an LLC?

Yes, but always seek professional legal and tax advice before you move any property into or out of any type of entity.

Can I convert a partnership or a limited partnership into an LLC?

Yes. In most states, a conversion to an LLC is fairly straightforward. However, seek appropriate legal and tax advice before taking action.

Are there any name restrictions on LLCs?

Yes. Each state has some restrictions on what types of names you can use for your LLC. In most cases, those restrictions don't interfere much. However, there are some commonsense things you may not want to do. If privacy is important, do not name your LLC after your family. Likewise, naming an LLC after the mailing address of a particular property, for example, is not advised because it causes mail delivery problems. Along those same lines, if you exchange the Main Street property and replace it with the property at 567 South Street, you end up with the 1234 Main Street LLC as the owner of 567 South Street.

Are there any disadvantages to LLCs?

Yes. Disadvantages include start-up costs, administrative costs, annual state fees, and the effort involved to maintain the entity. Still, those are far outweighed by the limited liability and asset protection advantages gained.

7 The Series LLC

A New Approach to LLCs

The newest and most exciting entity form for asset protection for real estate investments is the series LLC. If this cutting-edge entity is adopted in all states and all of the questions about taxation are answered, the series LLC will likely become the preferred entity for real estate investors. The concept behind the series LLC is that many separate cells or small LLCs all come under the umbrella of one organization. Each of the individual cells is separated for liability and asset protection purposes. This means that although there may be five or six cells under one umbrella LLC, the liability generated by one cell does not affect the others.

The first LLC legislation to allow the existence of series LLCs was in 1996 in Delaware. Delaware has almost always been a leader in developing new business entities, primarily because the Delaware courts, the Delaware legislature, and the Delaware political bodies are all business-friendly. The state's laws allow favorable privacy protection, and the state has courts specifically for business disputes. To understand how Delaware views the series LLC and the asset protection it provides, it is probably best to look at the act itself:

> [6del.C.section 18-215] The debts, liabilities, obligations, and expenses incurred, contracted for, or otherwise existing with respect to a particular series shall be enforceable against the assets of such series only and not against the assets of the company generally or any other series thereof as long as separate books and records are kept for each of the series.

With that statutory definition in mind, the series LLC appears to lend itself to multiple real estate investments. If you owned 30 apartment buildings across the country and you could put each of them into a different series of one LLC, you would significantly reduce the amount of administrative overhead and structure needed to protect yourself. In addition, you cut down the expenses of forming entities and of state and federal tax filings each year, because you do not have to prepare documents for a bunch of separate LLCs. In the series LLC, you would have all of the different series reporting to the main LLC, and conceptually it would, in turn, file only one tax return on behalf of all of the cells of the organization. All the while, your properties would be individually protected from the liabilities of all the others.

How a Series LLC Works

Interestingly, each series or cell individually can have different operating managers, different financial investors, and different profit distributions. A group of investors that wishes to buy multiple properties around the country and take in different investors for each property could place all of those varying properties under the one umbrella series LLC. The only qualification is that all of the accounts and debts must be segregated into each specific series. Here's an example:

A series LLC in Nevada is owned by Bob, Joe, and Wanda. These owners have four or five real estate investments throughout the country, and Bob, Joe, and Wanda have decided to do a subdivision in Texas. The subdivision in Texas will be headed up by Wanda's son, who is not currently a member (owner) of the LLC. A "Texas series" could be created under the umbrella Nevada series LLC by an amendment to the internal operating agreement. That operating agreement could name Wanda's son as the manager of the Texas series and make him part-owner of just that series.

The Texas series could take on investors in Texas, complete its subdivision, report its final figures to the master LLC, and then be dissolved. It could do all this without affecting or creating any liability for the other properties in the umbrella LLC or the principles who were uninvolved with the Texas venture.

Here's another example of how a series LLC might be very valuable as your entity structure:

Say you owned a number of restaurants throughout Oklahoma. On the one hand, you could file a separate LLC for each of the restaurants; however, the administrative headaches would multiply for each one you filed. On the other hand, the restaurant chain could file for a series LLC, and then each restaurant in a particular city could be a separate cell or separate series of the main organization. Because you have created these separate cells, if one restaurant goes out of business or becomes bankrupt, those leases, employee contracts, and ongoing landlord-tenant agreements will not create liability for the overall ownership or for any of the other restaurants (which, perhaps, are performing very well). It does not affect them—only the one cell collapses.

The LLC of the Future?

While series LLCs seem to be ideal and are the cutting edge, they are not widely used right now because there are many unanswered questions. Even states that have adopted series LLC legislation are still sorting some things out. Additionally, because only a limited number of states allow the formation of series LLCs, how the courts of other states will view their cell-style limited liability and asset protection features remains uncertain.

When the United States was formed, all of the states agreed that they would honor each other's laws. This applies to dealing with out-of-state business entities as well. Generally, the suggested course of action in most states is to look to law in the state of the entity's formation to determine how to deal with that entity. However, this is just a guideline—it is not required. Let's look at an example:

> Assume that you live and own property in Ohio and you create a Delaware series LLC because you cannot create a series LLC in Ohio, where there is no such entity. Ohio will allow you to do business in Ohio as a Delaware entity once you provide a *certificate of good standing* (which is simply a statement from Delaware saying that your LLC was formed properly and that you are in good standing in Delaware). However, if a lawsuit arises or a creditor pursues a judgment, will the Ohio courts honor the cell-like barriers established by your Delaware entity? The Ohio courts might have a problem with the idea that creditors doing business in Ohio are bound by Delaware's laws restricting them from being able to go after the assets of the other series in the LLC. In fact, the Ohio courts might decide to apply Ohio's LLC rules, which, of course, do not allow for the cellular structure of a series LLC. With this possibility in mind, a Delaware series LLC doing business in Ohio might not be afforded the same cellular protections it would receive under Delaware law.

There has yet to be a significant court ruling to give planners any guidance in this area, so for now it's an unsettled issue.

Similar concerns and issues arose when standard LLCs started coming into existence. The spread and acceptance of standard LLCs took about 19 years. Wyoming was the first state to enact LLC legislation in 1977, and the last state was Hawaii around 1996 when the Uniform Limited Liability Company Act came into existence. During that 19-year transitional acceptance period, few businesspeople were brave enough to take advantage of the LLC entity because of the same kind of unanswered concerns. Now, of course, all that's been resolved, and the LLC entity has established itself as one of the top three entity forms (corporations and limited partnerships being the other two). So how long do we have to wait for the series LLC to gain widespread acceptance? Hopefully not 19 years, but some states seem to have more motivation than others to resist. California, for example, charges a minimum annual fee, usually $800, for each entity doing business in the state of California. When asked for their position on series LLCs, the California state taxing entity (the Franchise Tax Board) had this to say (emphasis added):

> A Series LLC is essentially a master LLC that has separate divisions, similar to an S corporation with Q-subs. Each division has its own liabilities and assets and a creditor should only be able to pursue that entity's assets rather than the entire series' assets. The claimed business purposes are liability protection and flexibility, with the added bonus that they would pay the LLC fee and the minimum tax only once. . . . California has not adopted a statute similar to the Delaware Series LLC. Tax practitioners propose that only one Form 568 needs to be filed for the entire series. FTB does not agree. *Our current position is that each series in a Delaware Series LLC is considered a separate LLC and must file its own Form 568 Liability Company Return of Income and pay its own separate LLC annual tax and fee if it is registered or doing business in California.*

Thus, at least in California, each series in a series LLC is a separate tax-paying entity and must report and pay taxes to the state of California. Generally, this position by the Franchise Tax Board looks like bad news for the series LLC, because if you have a series LLC containing four separate cells or series, then you have to pay the minimum Franchise Tax Board tax of $800 (along with any gross proceeds tax) for each one. That is a minimum of $3,200 annual fee each year for your series LLC, which, by definition and purpose, should incur only $800 for the one main entity. Obviously, the state of California prefers to collect $800 on each one.

Nevertheless, California proponents of series LLCs consider this ruling progress. You may be wondering why; after all, isn't one of the main reasons for creating a series LLC to lessen the administrative headaches and the tax burdens of having separate LLCs? What California is saying is that it sees each of the cells in a series LLC as separate tax-paying entities. If that is the case, then it must also see each series in a series LLC as a separate entity for limiting liability and asset protection purposes. It would be difficult to argue that each series should be treated separately for taxes but not for asset protection. Further strengthening that argument, California's Franchise Tax Board's most recent tax publication (FTB Pub. 3556) for LLCs describes a series LLC as follows (emphasis added):

> A Series LLC is a single LLC that has separate allocations of assets each within its own series. *The laws under which Series LLCs are formed provide for special liability protections and member allocations for each series within the LLC.*
>
> For purposes of filing in California, each series within a Series LLC must file a separate Form 568, Limited Liability Company Return of Income, and pay its separate LLC annual tax and fee if it is registered or doing business in California, and both of the following apply:

- The holders of interest in each series are limited to the assets of that series upon redemption, liquidation, or termination, and may share in the income only of that series.
- Under state law, the payment of the expenses, charges, and *liabilities of each series is limited to assets of that series.*

Again, all of this language indicates that California recognizes the separateness, liability-limiting characteristics, and asset protection features of the individual series or cells within a series LLC. While it doesn't reduce the amount of minimum annual fees California will charge, it does indicate that a series LLC might be appropriate for real estate investors who have only one or two properties in California and perhaps properties scattered in other states. In that case, only series doing business in California would suffer multiple annual fees. Each state is going to have its own position. Hopefully your state is more business-friendly (tax-friendly) than California.

Formation Formalities

Although Delaware was the first state to allow series LLCs, several other states have enacted similar provisions allowing the series LLC structure. At the time of this writing, Delaware, Illinois, Iowa, Nevada, Oklahoma, Tennessee, and Utah all have series LLC legislation. The formation of a series LLC is a lot like the formation of a normal LLC, except that the articles of organization must specifically state that it is a "series LLC," and the operating agreement is likely to be much more complicated in that it needs to detail the structure and operation of each of the different series. The purpose of the series LLC statement in the articles of organization is to alert potential creditors that a cellular structure exists and that the assets and liabilities of each will be maintained as separate. It gives them fair notice that, as a creditor, they may be limited to just the assets of the series with which they are involved.

After filing the articles of organization with the state and adopting a series LLC operating agreement, creating or dissolving future series is just a matter of making an amendment or addendum to the operating agreement. There is no need to file or refile additional state documents. Once the umbrella series LLC exists, new cells can come into existence and be dissolved internally at the discretion of the LLC's management.

Cost to Create and Operate a Series LLC

The cost to create a series LLC is going to be a little more than that of a regular LLC. Primarily, the added expense is because of the uniqueness and complexity of the operating agreement. Likewise, only some states allow the formation of a series LLC, and if you're not in one of those states, registering your series LLC to do business in your own state will cost something. However, the cost of creating a series LLC is still less than paying for each entity individually. In the case of a series LLC, each new series can be created internally with a simple amendment or addendum to the operating agreement. This feature alone may make the series LLC an economical choice.

Piercing the Veil and Charging Order Issues of the Series LLC

In the previous chapter, we looked at the concept of "piercing the veil" and "charging orders" as they apply to LLCs. There's no sense in repeating that here, so if you didn't read those sections of that chapter, now would be a good time to backtrack. With those concepts in mind, the cell-like features of a series LLC would arguably have the same weaknesses and same strengths. However, because there is no uniform acceptance of the series LLC, how vigorously and evenhandedly courts in other states will enforce the intended liability-limiting and asset protection features between cells within the same series LLC is still an open question.

Series LLC Summary

As you've seen, the series LLC can be an excellent tool for real estate investors. Its key features include the following:

- One umbrella LLC contains a number of separate cells, or series.
- Each series or cell has its own assets and liabilities.
- Each series is liable only for its own debts and obligations.
- Creditors of one series may only reach the assets of that series.
- Each series can have its own members (owners) and may be managed separately from the umbrella series LLC and other cells.
- As with a regularly formed LLC, the members (owners) of each series are not financially responsible for the debts and obligations of the series.
- A series may contain real estate investments in the series LLC state or may contain properties scattered throughout the country, each separated as its own series.
- A series LLC can be formed in another state and operated in a state that has not adopted series LLC legislation.

If the concept of the series LLC moves across the country as the original LLC did and all states ratify series LLC statutes, then five to ten years from now, it will be the standard of practice and definitely the most advisable entity type. Once the kinks are worked out, the series LLC really will be the next best thing. Its ease of use in the internal formation and dissolution of different ventures, as well as its intended ability to reduce administrative headaches, make it ideal for the real estate investment community.

8 Limited Partnerships and Family Limited Partnerships

IN THIS CHAPTER, we will look at the various forms of partnerships. The first thing we will look at is general partnerships. A *general partnership* in regards to real estate investment is simply when a property is owned by two or more people in their own names. In almost all real estate investment situations, general partnerships should be avoided. Even so, the number of general partnerships in relation to other partnerships might be as high as 70 percent to 80 percent. Presumably, if you're reading this book, you've already realized that some type of structure to provide limited liability and asset protection is a smart thing to do. General partnerships provide neither limited liability nor asset protection. Nevertheless, I know many people who read this book are already in some type of a general partnership, so we'll cover it briefly.

We'll also examine the various types of limited partnerships. Limited partnerships have some specialized uses, but generally speaking, most things that can be accomplished with a limited partnership can be better accomplished with a limited liability company (LLC).

With that said, the majority of this chapter will focus on family limited partnerships. Family limited partnerships have some unique and desirable features and are widely promoted as asset protection and estate tax–planning entities. We're going to spend some time focusing on both of those features as well as some of their drawbacks, IRS challenges, and the current state of law.

Partnerships

The formality for partnerships has a default. The default, or most basic form, of a partnership is that two people get together and buy a piece of property. They do not have any agreements; they might not have even had a handshake. Each one merely contributed a certain amount of money, they both qualified for the credit to purchase the property, and they both own it. They have a partnership. There is a structure to their partnership, even though they did not create the structure. By default, a thing called the Uniform Partnership Act dictates the structure. The Uniform Partnership Act was created because, among other reasons, a lot of people form partnerships in the way I just described. In fact, as important as it is, people rarely put on paper each partner's rights, responsibilities, profit distributions, and so on.

Sometimes partnerships that lack formal structure can grow into very big ventures. What started out as some scribbling on a cocktail napkin all of a sudden turns into a major subdivision worth millions of dollars. Without a formal structure, what happens if some kind of dispute arises between the partners? What happens if one of the partners dies? Without something in writing, there's nothing to say what their rights are and who gets what. Of course, by the time there is a problem, memories have faded, and nobody really recalls what the agreement was in the first place. Sometimes the dispute reaches a boiling point, and the dispute turns into litigation. Again, without a formal structure, how does the court know how to divide the partnership assets? Because of this, some standardized rules have been needed throughout history to determine each partner's rights in relation to others'.

The way to do that originally was through the courts. One partner had to sue another partner, and a judge had to decide what was what. But over time, that got cumbersome, and nobody wanted the uncertainty of having a judge preside over the dispute. You never knew which way a judge was going to decide. Eventually, the need arose to have a more standardized set of rules for partnerships.

In 1914, the first Uniform Partnership Act was created and adopted by most states. Since then, the Uniform Partnership Act has been revised a number of times, with the latest version enacted in 1997.

The Uniform Partnership Act creates a formal structure for those partnerships that do not have one to begin with. If you do not create a partnership agreement detailing the rights of the respective partners, your partnership is defined for you via the Uniform Partnership Act. It says what your rights are, what your responsibilities are, who does the books, who has the right to see those books, how often they can see the books, and all the other things that should have been determined at the formation of the partnership.

In many cases, the Uniform Partnership Act works just fine. For example, it assumes that if two partners put in equal money, then the profits are equal; if there was a skewing of investment, then there should be a skewing of profits in relation to the size of the investment. But what happens if you have a more complicated situation? Assume that one person is putting in money and one person is putting in effort. How do you compensate the effort? How do you compare a dollar's worth of investment to a dollar's worth of effort? If you are the person who put in the effort rather than the money, are you going to get your equal share based on the rules of the Uniform Partnership Act? You might not. It is always best to give some consideration to what you want. If you don't, then you'd better read the Uniform Partnership Act, because you're stuck with it.

Another problem with failing to structure your own partnership is that, by default, you get a general partnership. In a general partnership, all of the partners are general partners, and, therefore, all the partners are jointly and severally liable for the debts of the partnership. This means that if there is a judgment against the partnership and you have personal assets, but your partner doesn't, the attorneys will get the full judgment out of you. The partner without assets is off the hook. Granted your partner got off the hook because he had no assets to begin with, but is that going to make you feel any better when your assets are being seized to pay the whole judgment? Likewise, what if one of your partners has to declare bankruptcy? Then what happens to the assets of your partnership?

The point of listing these unpleasant possibilities is to reinforce that you should never have a partnership unless you take the time to set up a proper partnership structure.

Protect yourself by always having some type of formal structure that says whether you are liable and, if so, to what degree. If you don't want to be liable, have a partnership agreement that spells out that you are not responsible for the debts of the venture or partnership.

Limited Partnerships

A limited partnership is a business structure with one or more general partners and one or more limited partners. General partners manage the partnership interests and assume responsibility and liability for the debts and obligations of the partnership. Limited partners, on the other hand, are only liable to the extent of their investments in the partnership. Limited partners are entitled to their portion of the profits but have no liability for the partnership's debts or obligations. In return for limited liability, limited partners have to give up any management role and the ability to control the direction of the partnership. If they exercise too much control of the partnership, they lose their limited partnership status and become liable. For example, a limited partner cannot sign on a note. Signing on a note is an *active participation event;* that is, an act that says, "I am responsible for this partnership." A limited partner who takes such actions has lost her limited partner status—at least, that is what the plaintiff's lawyers would argue. If you are a limited partner, make sure to stay a limited partner.

Limited partnerships are still a viable business entity. However, because a limited partnership by definition has to have general partners who are still fully liable for the debts and liabilities of the partnership, a better choice is usually an LLC. Even in those cases where, for one reason or another, a limited partnership is preferred, it's recommended that an LLC be formed to act as a general partner. By having an LLC act as the general partner in a limited partnership, only the assets of the general partner LLC (which can be minimal) are exposed to liability from the limited partnership. It takes a very unusual set of circumstances to justify creating this kind of entity, because in most situations, the LLC alone would provide both limited liability and asset protection. Even if the goal were to make sure some partners have no say in management, an LLC operating agreement can be drafted to limit the participation of those persons. However, the one area where limited partnerships are still commonly used is in family limited partnerships.

Family Limited Partnerships

We have learned that a limited partnership is a partnership consisting of two classes of partners: general partners and limited partners. A general partner controls the partnership's assets and investments and manages the partnership business. A limited partner has interest in the partnership but only plays a passive role. A limited partner's exposure to liability for the debts of the limited partnership is limited to the amount of his investment in the partnership.

To maintain the limitation on her liability, the limited partner is prohibited from participating in any management or control over the partnership's assets or business. A limited partnership interest is intangible personal property, and, therefore, the interest is assignable and transferable by the limited partner subject to restrictions set forth in the partnership agreement. One can not be both a general partner and limited partner simultaneously.

A *family limited partnership* is sometimes abbreviated as FLP or referred to as a "flip." A family limited partnership is simply a limited partnership that is usually made up of members of an immediate family. There are no well-defined legal restrictions, so a family limited partnership can include extended family members as well. In a family limited partnership, one or both parents usually serve as the general partner, with their children and/or extended family members owning interests in the limited partnership. At formation, the parents typically own almost all of the limited partnership investment interests. Family limited partnerships are very popular entities, because they can be used to control family assets while reducing the value of an estate for estate tax purposes.

You won't find any IRS regulations referring to *family limited partnership* or references to the term in the Uniform Limited Partner Act. That's because the term *family limited partnership* evolved from the estate-planning legal community as a description of limited partnerships that are set up specifically to hold family businesses or investments. Nevertheless, *family limited partnership* has become well known and widely used.

Asset Protection Benefits of Family Limited Partnerships

As just mentioned above, a family limited partnership is simply a regular limited partnership with ownership distributed among a family. With that said, the liability that can flow from the assets or businesses owned by the family limited partnership is limited to the general partners. The limited partners have no personal liability. So that raises two questions: (1) is there a way to limit the general partner personal liability, and (2) are the assets of the family limited partnership safe from any debts incurred outside the FLP by the limited partners?

Limiting General Partner Liability. The general structure of a family limited partnership requires that at least one member of the partnership be the general partner. A general partner is, of course, liable for the debts of the partnership. With that in mind, it's somewhat unappealing to have the parents or older generation act as a general partner, because generally that is where the wealth is. Also unappealing, however, is to have the parents or older generation become limited partners because of the loss of control of the assets. To avoid both of these undesirable results, it's generally considered prudent to form an S corporation or LLC to act as the general partner.

The structure of the S corporation or LLC as the general partner should be such that the parents, acting through the general partner entity, still control the assets of the family limited partnership but avoid the liability problems of being a general partner. One common variation of this structure is for the parent to form or use an existing revocable trust as the general partner. This is not recommended, however, because a court can compel the parent to revoke the trust, thereby leaving the parent exposed as a general partner. Likewise, an entity (an S corporation or LLC) formed to act as the general partner that is wholly owned by the parents or the parents' revocable trust may have the same result. Thus, the structure of the entity acting as general partner for the family limited partnership must have a diversified underlying ownership. The possible combinations for structuring a family limited partnership with an additional liability protection entity to act as the general partner are beyond the scope of this book and should be explored in detail with your attorney.

Outside Debt Considerations for FLP Limited Partners. Another concern of most of my clients is that the limited partnership interests that they give or transfer to their children or extended family may become exposed to the creditor claims or spousal claims of that family member.

The interest of a limited partner in a family limited partnership is exposed to the creditor claims of the limited partner. However, reaching a limited partner's interest in a family limited partnership is difficult and unappealing for creditors.

Most states have adopted some form of the Uniform Limited Partnership Act (ULPA). The ULPA sets out the procedure that creditors must follow in pursuing any debtor's interest in a family limited partnership. Just as we saw in the chapter on limited liability companies, there is a clear distinction between a limited partner's interest in the partnership and the partnership's ownership of partnership property. Similar to a creditor of a member of an LLC, a creditor of a limited partner is not entitled to seize assets within the partnership to satisfy the debt of that limited partner. The ULPA was based on the basic business principle that it is more desirable to protect innocent partners' interests in a partnership than it is to permit the creditor of any one partner to satisfy a judgment by disrupting, or perhaps destroying, the partnership's business. In those states that have adopted some form of the ULPA, a creditor's only recourse against a limited partner's interest is a charging order.

Charging orders were covered in detail in Chapter 6. Applying that same methodology to family limited partnerships, we see that a creditor granted a charging order against one of the limited partners is limited to the rights given assignees of limited partnership interests. Under the ULPA, just as with LLCs, an assignee of a limited partner only gets the right to receive distributions of cash and other property from the partnership to that limited partner. The charging order is served on the partnership directing that all distributions due the debtor-partner must go to the creditor instead. Because a charging order is a court order, the family limited partnership has no choice; if and when money or property is to be distributed to the debtor partner, the partnership must instead deliver the money or property to the creditor. However, *if* and *when* distributions are to be made becomes very important. A well-drafted family limited partnership agreement gives the general partner the *sole* discretion as to if, when, and how much to distribute to the limited partners. The general partner may simply chose to refrain from making distributions when a partner has creditor problems, which means the creditor with the charging order would not get anything of value from the family limited partnership.

In some states, a creditor may also foreclose on a charging order. Foreclosure of a charging order actually allows the creditor to sell charged transferable interest to a purchaser. However, just as with LLC interests, the foreclosure doesn't give the purchaser any rights to participate in the management of the limited partnership's activities. The purchaser obtains nothing more than the status of a transferee. Because membership is presumably made up of friendly family members, there's not much of a market for foreclosed family limited partnership interests. And just as we saw in the LLC chapter, if a creditor has foreclosed on a charging order and the general partner does not distribute partnership income, the creditor/assignee, not the debtor-limited partner, is responsible to pay the tax on the allocated income. As a result, the creditor/assignee is saddled with the tax consequences resulting from partnership income without having the capacity to force distributions or dissolve the partnership. Obviously, given the limited nature of the charging order remedy and the potential exposure to partnership taxation without corresponding distributions, most creditors are reluctant to pursue a charging order judgment remedy against a debtor's interest in a limited partnership.

Other possible creditor deterrents that can sometimes be implemented are the so-called poison pill provisions. One such poison pill provision that can sometimes be included in family limited partnership agreements allows either the family limited partnership or other partners to buy out the debtor-member for a nominal amount. This poison pill has the effect of substituting the debtor-member's membership interest with a nominal amount of cash, which limits the assets a creditor can collect against. In some cases, poison pill provisions can eliminate the need for charging-order protection and can be especially effective when the family limited partnership is holding investment real estate.

Estate Tax Benefits of FLPs

One of the most powerful advantages of a family limited partnership is that it can help reduce the amount of gift and estate taxes. Each person qualifies for a certain amount of estate tax exemption. That exempt portion of an estate passes to the heir(s) without taxes. All amounts above the exemption are fully taxable. Estate taxes can reach as high as 45 percent. As I write this, the estate tax affects only people who die leaving a taxable estate of more than $2 million. There's a lot of speculation about what kind of changes will be enacted to replace the present estate tax exemption legislative scheme. Our present rules have an increasing exemption that reverts back to a lesser amount because of a built-in sunset provision. As it stands now, the estate tax threshold will continue to rise until 2010, when the tax will be repealed. The current rules are shown in Table 8.1.

If you have an estate in excess of the estate tax exemption, you have good reason for concern. A limited partnership can help in three ways:

1. Using your annual gift tax exclusion and gift tax exemption
2. Taking valuation discounts
3. Removing future appreciation from your estate

Let's look at an example:

> Steve and Mary own and operate two apartment buildings and a commercial property. Collectively, the three properties are valued at $2.5 million. Their total estate including these properties is approximately $7 million. Steve and Mary transfer

TABLE 8.1 *Estate and Gift Taxes*

Year	Estate Tax Exemption	Gift Tax Exemption	Highest Estate and Gift Tax Rate
2008	$2 million	$1 million	45%
2009	$3.5 million	$1 million	45%
2010	Estate tax repealed	$1 million	45% (gift tax only)
2011	$1 million	$1 million	55%

all three properties to a newly formed family limited partnership in exchange for a 2 percent general partnership interest and a 98 percent limited partnership interest in the FLP. Steve and Mary then make a one-time gift of 80 percent of their limited partnership interests to their four adult children (each child receives a 20 percent interest). An independent qualified appraiser values the FLP at $2.5 million and also determines that the value of the gifts of the limited partnership interest should be discounted by 15 percent to account for the lack of marketability and an additional 15 percent to account for the minority interest transferred to each child. Thus, the value of the one-time gift is determined to be $2,500,000 \times 0.80 \times 0.70 = \$1,400,000$. Steve and Mary also plan to gift the remaining limited partnership interests systematically to their grandchildren over a number of years, using their annual gift tax exclusions.

The above scenario incorporates all three of the estate and gift tax benefits of a family limited partnership. First, gifts of interests in a family limited partnership are subject to federal gift tax (and possibly state gift tax). However, every taxpayer (currently) has a $1 million lifetime exemption from the gift tax, so in the above example, the transfer to the children will be free from gift tax to the extent of the parents' available lifetime exemption. In addition, the example stated that they intended to gift limited partnership interests systematically to their grandchildren over time. Those transfers, if properly planned, will be free from gift tax under the annual gift tax exclusion (currently $12,000 per recipient).

Second, Steve and Mary should be able to discount the value of the FLP interests given away. That's because the limited partners have very restricted rights, such as (a) the inability to transfer interest, (b) the inability to withdraw from the FLP, and (c) the inability to participate in management. These restrictions can result in a business value that is significantly less than the value of the underlying assets. In our example, Steve and Mary had an independent qualified appraiser determine that the value of the gifts of the limited partnership interest should be discounted by 15 percent to account for the minority interest (lack of control) and an additional 15 percent to account for the lack of marketability of the interests transferred to each child. Thus, Steve and Mary were able to transfer $2 million of assets out of their estate at a gift tax value of $1.4 million.

Third, Steve and Mary have removed any future appreciation on those properties from their estate. Real estate assets generally appreciate over time. Distributing your assets among family members freezes the current value and keeps any growth in value out of your estate later.

Is estate planning really worth all this effort? Setting aside any future real estate appreciation or any future gifting to the grandchildren, Steve and Mary's one-time gift of limited partnership interests to their children has arguably already saved their estate $270,000. How? The FLP $2 million gift to their children was discounted to $1.4 million, effectively moving $600,000 out of their estate tax-free. The tax on the $600,000 otherwise would have been approximately $270,000. Once you start adding back in future real estate appreciation and the savings that will come from additional gifting to grandchildren, the numbers become very significant. So is it really worth all the effort? You decide.

Family Limited Partnerships Targeted by the IRS

Obviously, the IRS has never been happy with the idea of discounting family limited partnership interests. In recent years, the IRS has stepped up its resistance to discounting, and there have been cases where the discounts have been disallowed. However, those cases featured questionable business practices, and the discounts attempted were highly abusive.

One case that looked as though it might spell the end of family limited partnership discounting was *Estate of Albert Strangi v. Commissioner*. The facts of that case were as follows:

> Mr. Strangi, an 80-year-old man, was diagnosed as terminally ill with 18 to 24 months to live. Mr. Strangi's son-in-law, Michael Gulig, was handling his business affairs for him under a power of attorney. On August 11, 1994, Mr. Gulig attended a seminar about family limited partnerships, and the next day, he formed the Strangi Family Limited Partnership (SFLP) and a corporation to serve as the 1 percent general partner of the FLP.
>
> Mr. Strangi contributed property with a fair market value of approximately $11 million to the FLP in exchange for a 99 percent limited partnership interest. The property contributed by Mr. Strangi represented approximately 98 percent of his wealth and included his personal residence and other real estate, cash, securities, accrued interest and dividends, insurance policies, an annuity, and partnership interests. Approximately 75 percent of that value was attributable to cash and securities. He then purchased 47 percent of the corporation serving as general partner, and his four children purchased the other 53 percent. Mr. Gulig was appointed the managing director of the partnership interests with the power to control the timing and the amount of any distributions from the partnership.
>
> Numerous payments were made for Mr. Strangi's benefit—including for some of his personal in-home health care expenses

as well as for back surgery for a nurse who was injured while caring for Strangi. Mr. Strangi died two months after formation of the Strangi family limited partnership. The estate tax return was filed by Mr. Gulig. On that estate tax return, Mr. Strangi's interest in the Strangi Family Limited Partnership was valued at $6,560,730. This value was based on an appraisal of the Strangi Family Limited Partnership as an ongoing business. The appraisal discounted the interest's market value for a "minority interest" and for lack of marketability. The property held by the Strangi Family Limited Partnership prior to the discounts had a fair market value of $11,100,922.

The IRS immediately challenged the size of the estate's discount and also claimed that the full amount of the limited partnership interests should be included in Strangi's estate for federal estate taxes. The IRS argued Section 2036(a) of the Internal Revenue Code, which provides that transferred assets can still be included in the taxable estate if, prior to death, the decedent retained (1) possession or enjoyment of the assets or (2) the right to designate persons who shall possess or enjoy the assets.

Under the specific facts of the Strangi case, various payments were made from the Strangi Family Limited Partnership, both before and after Mr. Strangi's death, to meet Mr. Strangi's needs and expenses. Additionally, although Mr. Strangi transferred his house to the Strangi Family Limited Partnership, he continued to live there rent-free. The court found that he transferred so many of his assets into the Strangi Family Limited Partnership, he didn't even keep enough to meet his personal living expenses for his remaining life expectancy. Given the egregious facts in this case, the tax court ruled that the full, undiscounted value of the assets transferred to the Strangi Family Limited Partnership should be included in Mr. Strangi's estate for estate tax purposes. The *Strangi* decision was a big win for the IRS.

However, since the *Strangi* case decision, two major decisions have gone against the IRS: *Estate of Eugene E. Stone III v. Commissioner* and *Kimbell v. U.S.* The facts in both *Stone* and *Kimbell* were more easily interpreted as having a reasonable business purpose, so the courts sided with the taxpayer's estate.

So where does that leave us now? The general consensus is that family limited partnerships that are properly formed, funded, and operated will withstand IRS scrutiny and continue to provide an efficient way to transfer wealth to younger generations.

Some of the important lessons that came from the *Stone* and *Kimbell* cases are that the following can help support the validity of your family limited partnership:

- Always make sure your family limited partnership has a valid business purpose.
- Keep thorough, businesslike records.
- Create the FLP while you're still in good health.
- Observe all legal formalities when creating the FLP and while operating the business.
- Treat the FLP as a business entity, not a family trust.
- Hire an independent appraiser to value assets going into the FLP.
- Transfer legal title of assets going into the FLP.
- Put only business assets into the FLP; do not include a personal residence.
- Don't commingle FLP assets and personal assets.
- Never use FLP assets for personal purposes.
- Have a good operating agreement.
- Keep enough assets outside the FLP to pay for personal expenses.
- Distribute income to partners pro rata.

This is one of those situations where the old saying, "Pigs get fed, but hogs get slaughtered," really applies. There is ample, well-established, law that supports the reasonable discounting of limited partnership interests, but if you go overboard, you'll quickly find out the IRS is watching. So what's considered a "reasonable" discount percentage? In FLPs that own and operate real estate investments, a 25 percent to 40 percent discount is not unreasonable.

Before you start calculating how much money discounting will save you, you need to start by making sure that your family limited partnership qualifies for discounting at all. An FLP is subject to more restrictive rules than other forms of business entities. It's especially important that care be taken to create a valid FLP in the eyes of the state and the IRS. An FLP will be recognized only if it is formed for a valid business purpose. The FLP form will be disregarded if the IRS or the state finds that it was formed solely to avoid taxes. In fact, the IRS has enacted certain rules to prevent taxpayers from using the FLP form as a means to split family income and circumvent taxes. The following six factors must be satisfied for an entity to qualify as a valid FLP:

1. Distributions of interests in an FLP must be to family members only.
2. Reasonable compensation must be paid to partners who actually work for the partnership.
3. FLP income distributed to a partner can't be disproportionately greater than the capital contributed by that partner.
4. Partners must receive partnership interests through a bona fide transaction (gift or sale).
5. The FLP must own income-producing assets (e.g., real estate).
6. All formalities of existence must be observed.

Family limited partnerships are not for everyone. However, they can provide significant asset protection, family succession planning, and potential estate tax reduction opportunities. For families who wish to transfer control of substantial assets in an orderly, tax-favorable manner, family limited partnerships may be the best option. Likewise, families that operate significant residential rental properties or commercial real estate are usually in a strong position to take advantage of the potential partnership interest discounting.

9 Incorporating in Another State

ONE OPTION YOU have in creating an entity is to use the laws of another state. Many promoters suggest the laws of one state or another may be more favorable for different entity types. Along those same lines, each state has differing filing requirements, filing costs, degrees of privacy, and level of taxation. You may find that a state other than the one in which you live has more flexible rules or offers some advantage based on how you intend to form or operate your entity. In some cases, those differences may make it worthwhile for you to form your entity in that state.

Some states strive to be business-friendly and are constantly enacting more flexible entity legislation. Staying abreast of the current needs of business allows them to be forerunners in this area and attract more people to form businesses (entities) in their state. Entity formation seminars and online services often try to put a sales spin on these differences to enhance their marketing efforts. In this chapter, we'll take a look at some of these marketing claims to see if we can separate the truth from the hype.

The two states that are commonly touted as being business-friendly are Delaware and Nevada. This is not to suggest that other states are unfriendly to business, but Delaware and Nevada get the most publicity. If you go on the Internet and type into any search engine "incorporating in Delaware" or "incorporating in Nevada," you will get a list of Web sites that all have reasons why it is better to incorporate in one state versus another. For example, on Google, I got 12,700 search results for "incorporating in Delaware." The level of marketing and the number of gimmicks out there are approaching mind-boggling proportions with circuslike characteristics. Unfortunately, in a race to compete with each other, sometimes these promoters fail to update their information or makes claims that go a little beyond reality. So let's take a look at these two highly touted states and some of the various claims being made about them.

Delaware

- *The claim:* Delaware has a separate Court of Chancery for dealing with business affairs. This means that, unlike many states, the judges are specialized; the same judge who presides over criminal trials does not preside over business liability issues. It also means that the courts can rely on a large body of legal precedent, and often lawsuits are simply avoided because people have clear guidelines and more certainty in their business dealings.

    The reality: True, but not necessarily helpful. The Court of Chancery is great for those businesses operating in Delaware or large corporations that can contractually choose to have disputes heard in Delaware. Unfortunately, this doesn't really help you if you're doing business in another state, because if a suit is brought against you, it will be filed in your home state. Whatever state you actually operate in will require you to register to do business in that state. In registering to do business, you agree to be bound by that state's laws.

- *The claim:* Delaware legislation allows for the formation of a series LLC. Since Delaware law specifically allows the series LLC, other states allow the entity type because they must "look to" Delaware law in determining how to deal with series LLCs.

    The reality: Not true. Generally, states agree that each state will respect the laws of other states. With that said, your home state is supposed to look to the state of formation for how to base its rulings. However, that agreement between states is a guideline and is not required. In situations where there appears to be inherent unfairness in following another state's rules, the courts in your state may apply their own rules, and your asset protection barriers between cells in your series LLC may be set aside. The series LLC is just simply too new for an investor to rely on any of these marketing claims.

- *The claim:* Delaware's initial filing fees and annual business taxes are low. There is no income tax for Delaware entities that operate outside of Delaware. Delaware has no sales or personal property tax.

    The reality: True, with a catch. Delaware is one of those states that strives to attract new businesses. However, if you operate in a another state, you will still be subject to that state's income tax, franchise tax, property tax, sales tax, and filing fees when you register to do business in that state. The above claim makes it seem as though you are going to avoid all those taxes and fees when that is definitely not the case.

- *The claim:* Delaware allows single-member LLCs and one-person corporations.

    The reality: True. This is an advantage because some states do not allow single-member entities. If you're in one of those states, that may be a good reason to justify forming your business entity in another state.

- *The claim:* Delaware business regulations allow a higher degree of privacy and anonymity.

    The reality: True, sometimes. If privacy and anonymity are of utmost concern for you, then Delaware offers valid advantages. Keep in mind, however, that your operating state may still require you disclose your members, officers, shareholders, etc. when you register as a foreign entity doing business in the state. If so, it would nullify the privacy afforded you by the state of Delaware.

- *The claim:* Delaware allows your corporation to have asset protection.

    The reality: True, but so what? All properly formed corporations in any state are afforded asset protection. This is no reason to incorporate in Delaware over anywhere else.

- *The claim:* Corporations provide a major source of income for the state of Delaware, so the state maintains a very business-friendly atmosphere.

    The reality: True. There probably is a business-friendly climate, but if you operate in a different state, you must still deal with your state's department of corporations.

Nevada

- *The claim:* Nevada has no corporate income tax, no franchise tax, no taxes on shares, no personal income tax, and inexpensive annual fees.

    The reality: True. But again, it does not matter if the incorporation state has little to no taxes or fees. These things will still be payable in your operating state if it requires them.

- *The claim:* Nevada is superior because it doesn't share information with the IRS.

    The reality: Of course it doesn't! There's no state income tax, so what information would the state share? Nevertheless, this is touted as one of the main benefits for Nevada business entities. Again, if you do business in another state, you will need to register to do business in that state, and it likely will have an information-sharing agreement with the IRS.

- *The claim:* Stockholders are not of public record.

    The reality: Not true. While you will see this claim listed on many Web sites, as of 2005, the business registration form for Nevada requires that you list the name(s) and other information of the owner(s).

- *The claim:* Stockholders, directors, and officers do not have to be residents of or hold meetings in Nevada, and they do not have to be U.S. citizens.

    The reality: True. The first part of this statement is common to all states. Just because you have a corporation in a state doesn't mean that you actually have to hold meetings there. The second part of that sentence is where it gets important. Not all states allow noncitizens to form corporations, but Nevada does. However, keep in mind that for a corporation to qualify for a subchapter S election, the IRS requires all shareholders be U.S. citizens.

- *The claim:* Nevada corporate regulations make it harder to "pierce the corporate veil." This means that Nevada's courts very rarely find that a fully formed corporation does not protect the personal assets of the owners. In some other states, it is easier for a lawsuit to break through the bounds of your entity and come after your personal assets.

    The reality: True. The whole point of creating an entity is to shield your personal assets, so if the Nevada courts give better protection, then it's worth considering. What if you're sued in your own state? When an attack is based on the *structure* of your entity, most courts in other states will apply the interpretation and laws of the state of incorporation.

I want to point out that the term *Nevada corporations* is getting a very bad reputation. The traveling seminar people have found ways to abuse Nevada's business-friendly incorporation features. An abundance of seminars claim to show attendees how to use a Nevada corporation to acquire corporate credit, hide assets, and avoid taxes. In fact, thousands (maybe tens of thousands) of Nevada corporations have been formed for reasons other than legitimate business purposes. Most state taxing entities and the IRS are thought to pay closer attention to Nevada corporations because of the tremendous amount of abuse. At the present time, many legal practitioners feel that forming an entity in Nevada increases your risk for audit. Similarly, new Nevada corporations are thought to encounter more resistance when establishing credit lines. I have not seen hard facts on this, but have heard it said often enough to warrant consideration. In Nevada's defense, the state did nothing to create this negative reputation and is consistently ranked in the top three or four among business-friendly states.

Although there are some specialty reasons one might want to choose another state in which to form an entity, most legal practitioners, myself included, recommend staying with your home state. Dealing with the laws of another state along with having to register to do business in your home state just seems to add another, unnecessary layer of government paperwork to your busy life.

10 Domestic Asset Protection Trusts and Land Trusts

What Is an Asset Protection Trust?

One of the newest asset protection entities currently gaining marketing momentum is the domestic asset protection trust. A number of states have enacted legislation to allow domestic asset protection trusts, but the three getting the most press are Alaska, Delaware, and Nevada. That's why domestic asset protection trusts are also sometimes called "Alaska trusts," "Delaware trusts," or "Nevada trusts." Let's take a look at what benefits they may offer.

A domestic asset protection trust (DAPT) is also known as an irrevocable self-settled spendthrift trust. The *self-settled* portion of this name refers to any trust that is established for your own benefit. Living trusts are an example of this. You create a living trust with the intention that it will allow your estate to bypass the probate process, therefore preserving a significant portion of your estate's value for your spouse, children, or other beneficiaries. It benefits you (if you are the surviving spouse) or your beneficiaries, so it is considered self-settled. The *spendthrift* portion of the name refers to provisions within the trust that restrict access and specify that the trust contents are not subject to creditor claims. This spendthrift provision is touted as providing asset protection benefits.

Domestic asset protection trusts are allowed in only a handful of states. Asset protection trusts were first popular in offshore locations, but some states enacted domestic asset protection trust laws as a way to bring trust capital into their state.

Asset protection trusts consist of a grantor (the person making the trust), a trustee (the person in control of the trust), and beneficiaries. The grantor establishes the trust with a lawyer and names a trustee who will be in charge of the contents, the investments, and the distributions of the trust assets. Often, there is also a trust "protector" who has the power to veto any decisions made by the trustee regarding the handling of the trust assets. The most appealing part of this whole entity is that the grantor is also a beneficiary. The grantor no longer has overt control over the assets, but can still receive distributions made by the trustee from the trust. The theory is that the assets are protected from creditor claims because the grantor no longer owns them. However, because the grantor is a beneficiary named in the trust, she still has the right to distributions from the trust.

While the laws on domestic asset protection trusts vary among the states that allow them, the following are some common requirements they all share:

- The trust must be irrevocable, and the grantor cannot have control over the trust assets.
- The trustee must be a resident of the state in which the trust is established. The trustee can be a corporation hired to perform that task, but if so, the trustee/corporation must be doing business in the state.
- Some trust assets must be located in the state. If nothing is located in the state, some assets must be deposited there.
- The written trust agreement must specifically include spendthrift provisions.
- Transfers into the trust cannot be fraudulent transfers.

Most of these provisions are pretty straightforward, but it is necessary to explain the fraudulent transfer provision. A *fraudulent transfer* is any transfer of assets into the trust that serves to avoid known or *foreseeable* creditor claims. It is important to understand that fraudulent transfers are pretty loosely defined; merely circumstantial evidence can show your intent to defraud a creditor. Even if you had no intention of defrauding anyone, a judge could still rule that your transfer timing was intentional and fraudulent.

All states that allow asset protection trusts have also established time frames that limit a creditor's ability to challenge a transfer as a fraudulent transfer. In Delaware, for example, transfers to a trust cannot be challenged by a creditor after four years from the date of the transfer. Transfers within that four-year period, however, are at risk.

Is a DAPT Appropriate for Real Estate Investments?

As a real estate investor, you need to consider if an asset protection trust is even a viable option. Once your investments are transferred into the trust, only the trustee can make distributions or control the assets. In most situations, this loss of control makes domestic asset protection trusts unpalatable, but unfortunately, that's exactly what's required for the trust to retain its asset protection characteristics.

Problems With DAPTs

As a California attorney, I have never created an asset protection trust for a client, nor am I likely to, given their current status. It may seem like a potential option for your asset protection plan, but it offers limited protection at best. The biggest drawback of asset protection trusts is that they have become popular with the mass-market seminar promoters. All the recent publicity has drawn the attention and criticism of lawmakers, who see them as primarily a vehicle to defraud creditors. In fact, lawmakers recently amended the federal bankruptcy regulations to include a stipulation specifically regarding the asset protection trust.

The new regulation states that the statute of limitations for fraudulent transfers in bankruptcy situations is ten years. This is a very long time. For most people, there is no way to predict ten years in advance what one's financial situation may be, but if you put assets into an asset protection trust and then file for bankruptcy nine years later, that transfer could be considered fraudulent and all of the assets transferred at that time could be attached to the bankruptcy.

If you have no fear of bankruptcy and still feel that a domestic asset protection trust is a viable option for you, then you will still want to consider some of the other drawbacks. One of these is that state courts are held to the "full faith and credit" law. This means that the court of one state must uphold the decisions of the courts of all other states. How does this apply to asset protection trusts? Let's take a look at an example:

> Robert has a Nevada asset protection trust. If a creditor wanted to attack the trust itself, that creditor would have to bring the case to Nevada. Likely, Nevada will uphold its asset protection trust laws, and the creditor would be out of luck. However, even though the trust is in Nevada and the trustee is in Nevada, there are assets in Tennessee, and Robert, the grantor/beneficiary, is also in Tennessee. The creditor decides to attack the assets (not the trust) in a Tennessee court. The Tennessee judge sees a Tennessee resident, Tennessee property, and a Tennessee creditor and finds absolutely no reason to apply a Nevada law to this case; after all, no one is attacking the actual trust entity. The Tennessee judge orders the assets be turned over to the creditor.
>
> Now Robert does not technically have control over those assets—the trustee in Nevada does. Can the Tennessee judge then order the Nevada trustee to turn over those assets? Technically, no. However, all the creditor arguably has to do is take that judgment to the Nevada court and because of full faith and credit, the Nevada

judge must uphold the Tennessee ruling. The Nevada judge then orders the Nevada trustee to turn over the assets.

Another big problem with domestic asset protection trusts, unlike foreign trusts, is that the trustee is subject to U.S. court rulings. If in our above example, Robert's trust had been in the Cayman Islands, for instance, his trustee would also have been in the Cayman Islands and would not have had to listen to the Tennessee judge due to full faith and credit. If the trustee is not under U.S. jurisdiction, then the trustee cannot be forced to turn anything over. Does this mean foreign asset protection trusts are worth considering? Not if the trust is going to hold U.S. real estate assets. U.S. courts do not take kindly to a foreign trust or trustee refusing a court order regarding real estate within U.S. sovereign territory. So foreign asset protection trusts are no better in the context of holding (and protecting) real estate assets.

Hopefully, you see that asset protection trusts, whether domestic or foreign, are unlikely to stop creditors from attacking your assets unless you fit into a very narrow set of circumstances. The only people who should even begin to consider this option are those who are residents of a state with domestic asset protection trust laws, have all of their assets in that state, and have their trustee in that state. Even if all of that is in place, there are still more effective ways of protecting your assets and investments.

Land Trusts

A land trust is a revocable trust primarily used for privacy. In a land trust, the trustee takes title to the property in a way that ensures that the beneficiaries (true owners) cannot be easily discovered. The land trust agreement provides that the trustee—usually an attorney, bank, or independent trust company—agrees to hold ownership of a piece of real property for the benefit of the beneficiaries. Generally, the trust agreement stipulates that the trustee can perform one of four actions regarding the property: sell, buy, lease, or mortgage. It also stipulates that these actions can be performed only upon written direction of the beneficiary. The theory is that the beneficiaries (the true owners) still control the property and get the use, income, and benefits from it but their names never appear on property records. Generally, there is no state requirement to register a revocable trust, so there are no public records that would indicate the names of the beneficiaries. Even the private records held by the trustee are not accessible without a subpoena. Because of this, land trusts may be superior to other business entity forms if your primary goal is privacy. Currently only five states—Illinois, Florida, Georgia, Virginia, and North Dakota—have specific legislation allowing land trusts, but most other states allow foreign trusts to hold property within their territory.

11 Offshore and Other Exotic Asset Protection Planning

ONE OF THE sizzling topics in asset protection is offshore asset protection planning. I call it "sizzling" because both the traveling seminar people and Internet planning gurus are trying to sell you on it, while the IRS is issuing some very strongly worded warnings. There may be some very valid reasons to do offshore asset protection planning. Furthermore, there may be some very strong asset protection rules in other foreign jurisdictions that seem appealing. However, offshore asset protection planning has come under the scrutiny of the IRS because of what they perceive to be widespread abuse. In most cases, the offshore proponents are focused on what they call "tax avoidance," while the IRS is focused on what it calls "tax evasion."

As a real estate investor, there are three good reasons why you would *not* want to use offshore asset protection planning:

1. Real estate investments represent land and buildings (presumably) located somewhere in U.S. territory. State or federal courts do not take kindly to a foreign jurisdiction's attempt to restrict or limit their authority over assets located within their own territory.

2. There are many ways to limit liability and protect assets for real estate investments within the laws of our own country; there is simply no need to consider any kind of offshore or exotic asset protection planning.
3. The IRS is so fixated on any kind of offshore planning that anything along those lines is likely to earn you an audit.

The IRS has also deemed a number of domestic trusts and other creative planning techniques worthy of a closer look. Even if your intention has nothing to do with tax avoidance, the IRS won't know that until after it's audited you. With this in mind, you would be well advised to steer clear of some of the more extravagant plans being marketed on the Internet and through seminars. Sales pitches for many of these plans start by talking about asset protection concepts and then segue into tax strategies. The IRS is very serious about stopping this activity, and its Web site (IRS.gov) lists many of these abusive practices and gives fair warning. Nevertheless, some people ignore that warning. Here are some examples right off the IRS's Web site of what happens to some of the more creative planners (emphasis added):

Financial Guru and Wife Sentenced for Failing to Report Millions in Income; Obstruction of Justice

On August 2, 2007, in Seattle, WA, Wade B. Cook and his wife, Laura M. Cook, were sentenced to 88 months in prison and 18 months in prison, respectively. In addition, both are responsible for more than $3.7 million in restitution to the IRS. In February 2007, Wade Cook was convicted of tax evasion, filing false and fraudulent tax returns, and obstruction of justice. According to court documents, *Cook organized and lectured at hundreds of seminars on a wide range of financial and asset protection topics.* He also authored many books including *Wall Street Money Machine, Wealth 101, Brilliant Deductions,* and *Business by the Bible.* Testimony at trial revealed that in 1998, 1999, and 2000, Cook reported adjusted gross income of approximately $350,000. However, the government presented evidence that he did not report, and he willfully concealed, the receipt of approximately $9.5 million in royalties from his many books and seminars. As part of the tax fraud, Cook created a fictitious limited partnership called Never Ending Wealth, LP, which was in turn ostensibly owned by a type of tax exempt entity called a charitable remainder trust. Purportedly, the trust was for the benefit of the Mormon Church. In truth, the trust was simply a vehicle for Cook to fraudulently conceal his royalty income. No funds were left in the trust for the church. The jury also convicted Cook of obstruction of justice in connection with efforts to recharacterize use of the royalty funds, after the fact, as loans. In 2005, in a meeting with government prosecutors, a promissory note was produced dated March 1999, in an effort to show that the raiding of the trust account had been loans all along. Using computer forensics, the government showed the note had actually been typed by Laura Cook in 2003. Laura Cook pleaded guilty to obstruction of justice in April 2007.

Promoter of Abusive Trust Arrangements Sentenced to 87 Months in Prison

On October 1, 2007, in Raleigh, N.C., Howell W. Woltz, president of Sterling Trust Ltd. in Nassau, Bahamas, was sentenced to 87 months in prison, to be followed by three years of supervised release. Woltz pleaded guilty to tax fraud and money laundering charges. According to his plea agreement, *Woltz promoted offshore "dual trust" arrangements* to individuals in the United States for the purpose of evading federal income taxes. As part of these arrangements, customers opened offshore bank and debit card accounts. From on or about September 23, 2004, through March 2005, approximately $20 million was transferred to offshore bank accounts controlled by entities in Anguilla created by Woltz and his wife through Sterling Trusts Ltd. Woltz admitted he knowingly laundered or caused to be laundered approximately $7 million for his clients.

Minnesota Woman Sentenced for Tax Evasion

On September 27, 2007, in Minneapolis, Minn., Karen Jean Petersen was sentenced to 33 months in prison, to be followed by three years of supervised release, and ordered to pay a $7,500 fine. Petersen and her husband, Charles, were indicted in March 2005. According to the indictment, Petersen concealed the source of her business income and expenses by, among other methods, conducting her financial affairs through sham trusts, titling assets in the names of the sham trust, and conducting financial affairs in cash. In 1984, the Petersens formed the Pursue Enterprises Trust, which purportedly was the legal entity performing the house framing work of Charles Petersen. In an attempt to leave no records of business income or expenses, checks for the work done by Charles Petersen were made payable by home building general contractors to Pursue Enterprises. The Petersens, acting as the Trust, would negotiate checks for cash, and then use the money to purchase postal money orders for payment of personal and business expenses. The Petersens also conspired to evade taxes and conspired to fail to file federal income tax returns for calendar years 1989 through 1995. Following an IRS audit in 1996, the Petersens were assessed $181,563 in back taxes, interest, and penalties due to their evasion. On March 2006 the Petersens were convicted by a jury on charges of conspiracy to evade taxes and conspiracy to fail to file tax returns. After their convictions, Charles and Karen Petersen failed to appear at a scheduled sentencing hearing and remained fugitives until their arrest by U.S. Marshals on December 6, 2006. Charles Petersen died before he could be sentenced.

Tax Return Preparer Who Marketed Use of "Common Law Trusts" Sentenced to 151 Months in Prison

On July 20, 2007, in Miami, FL, Louis Wayne Ratfield, a former Lake Worth, FL, tax return preparer was sentenced to 151 months in prison, to be followed by five years of supervised release, and ordered to pay $40,000 for the costs of prosecution. On April 30, 2007, a federal jury convicted Ratfield of 50 counts associated with a tax fraud scheme. The evidence at trial established that Ratfield operated a tax preparation business, LWR Accounting and Tax Service, which was later called LWR Financial Services Trust. The evidence further established that Ratfield provided advice to clients on setting up and using "common law trusts" to claim deductions for ordinary living expenses on their returns to which they were not lawfully entitled, such as the costs of utilities, food, clothing, vehicles and education. *Ratfield marketed "common law trust" packages to clients throughout the United States via group seminars* and individual client meetings; sold over 100 trust packages at prices ranging from $2,995 to $5,995 each; and prepared at least 252 federal tax returns in connection with the scheme.

Self-Proclaimed CPA Sentenced for Role in Tax and Investment Fraud Scheme

On February 26, 2007, in Salt Lake City, UT, Lanny R. White was sentenced to 60 months in prison, [followed by] three years of supervised release, and ordered to pay more than $5 million in restitution. White pleaded guilty to fraud charges in November 2006 in connection with the promotion of a tax and investment fraud scheme. According to the plea agreement, White admitted that from 1993 to 2004, he and his co-conspirators—using the names Advanta Strategies, World Contractual Services, Rockwell Services, CornerStone West, Ventures Limited, and Whiven Financial—*marketed and sold a fraudulent trust scheme through seminars, promotional materials, and opinion letters.* White and his co-conspirators falsely represented to clients that by placing their businesses and assets into the names of trusts, the clients could lawfully eliminate or substantially reduce their income tax liabilities. Additionally, White admitted that, as part of his role in the conspiracy, he falsely claimed to be a licensed CPA and used his brother's CPA license number, without his brother's knowledge. White also admitted to preparing opinion letters that falsely assured the legality of the tax benefits of the fraudulent trust scheme and that he promoted the scheme at offshore seminars hosted by the Institute of Global Prosperity. White acknowledged that his actions, which resulted in the filing of more than 2,000 false and fraudulent federal income and trust tax returns, caused a loss of federal tax revenue totaling between $7 and $10 million. White also admitted to placing client's assets in unsound "investments" in international financial markets and other offshore "investing opportunities" that he knew would put clients' funds at considerable risk and would never, in fact, pay any return.

Defendant Gets 63 Months in Prison for Use of Fraudulent Trust Arrangements to Evade Taxes

On December 13, 2006, in Sacramento, CA, Charles Sigerseth, former owner of Sigerseth Insurance Agency, was sentenced to 63 months in federal prison on income tax charges. Sigerseth was also sentenced to three years of supervised release and was ordered to pay a $300 assessment. According to evidence introduced at trial, *Sigerseth attended a seminar put on by a company called National Trust Services* who told him that by putting his business into a "business trust" and directing all business profits to a "family trust," he could write off all personal expenses as business deductions on the family trust returns. Further, he was told, any remaining taxable income could be "set aside" into a "family foundation" that would purportedly later be donated to charity and that, as a result, the "set-aside" amount constituted a charitable deduction. Sigerseth implemented this scheme and used it for his 1993–1997 tax returns, usually paying just 10% of what he actually owed in federal taxes.

Creativity Consultant Gets Prison for Getting Creative with Tax Return

On November 3, 2006, in Buffalo, NY, Dr. Roger Firestien was sentenced to 15 months in prison, followed by two years supervised release, fined $5,000, and ordered to pay the costs of his incarceration. Firestien pleaded guilty in May to one count of willfully evading his 1998 income taxes. In December 2004, Firestien was indicted and charged with five counts of tax evasion and one count of filing a false tax return. The indictment alleged that *Firestien was a consultant, author, speaker, and writer in the field of creative problem solving.* In December 1997, Firestien purchased a Complex Business Organization (CBO) from an entity called Andersons Ark and Associates (AAA). The CBO was a business structuring plan designed to assist Firestien in evading his income taxes. Using the CBO, Firestien converted his sole proprietorship into an S Corporation called Innovation Resources, Inc., that was incorporated in New York State. He also created a partnership in Nevada called Innovation Resources, Ltd., in which he listed himself as a 5 percent partner and an AAA entity called Sawtooth Enterprises as a 95 percent partner. The purpose of forming this partnership was to fraudulently reduce Firestien's taxable income by creating business deductions that shifted a portion of his income to a nominee, Sawtooth. Firestien paid AAA a 5 percent fee to send some of the money that he deducted as business expenses to an account in Costa Rica that he accessed using a Visa debit card. According to the statement of facts in the plea agreement,

Firestien falsely deducted $132,700 in marketing and management expenses on tax returns filed with the IRS in April 1999. As a result of these filings, Firestien evaded approximately $48,126 in taxes for 1998. According to the government's calculation, the tax loss associated with these false filings and others associated with this scheme ranged from $120,000 to $200,000. To date, more than 30 people throughout the United States have been prosecuted in connection with the AAA scheme, including at least 21 clients such as Firestien.

Many more of these examples are available on the IRS's Web site. Many of these plans started out as a seminar marketed as some type of offshore or exotic asset protection and tax-planning seminar. The IRS prosecuted each of the examples above, so the focus of those articles is on tax evasion. Nevertheless, many people who attended those seminars and perhaps became involved with these companies did so for asset protection reasons, not tax planning. Unfortunately, it's hard to imagine that the quality of the asset protection advice was any better than the quality of a tax-planning advice.

My advice to clients is to avoid getting caught up in the marketing of these plans. The promoters are rarely ever attorneys, accountants, or other professionals who are actually qualified to provide advice. Basic business planning and common sense are always the best way to approach limiting liability and asset protection.

Appendix A

State Contact Information

Alabama
www.sos.state.al.us/business/corporations.aspx

Alaska
www.dced.state.ak.us/occ/

Arizona
www.azcc.gov/divisions/corporations/

Arkansas
www.sosweb.state.ar.us/corp_ucc.html

California
www.sos.ca.gov/business/business.htm

Colorado
www.sos.state.co.us/pubs/business/main.htm

Connecticut
www.concord-sots.ct.gov/CONCORD/index.jsp

Delaware
www.corp.delaware.gov

Florida
www.sunbiz.org

Georgia
http://sos.georgia.gov/corporations/

Hawaii
www.hawaii.gov/dcca/areas/breg/registration/

Idaho
www.idsos.state.id.us/corp/corindex.htm

Illinois
www.cyberdriveillinois.com/departments/business_services/

Indiana
www.in.gov/sos/business/corporations.html

Iowa
www.sos.state.ia.us/business/index.html

Kansas
www.kssos.org/business/business.html

Kentucky
www.sos.ky.gov/business/

Louisiana
www.sos.louisiana.gov/tabid/98/Default.aspx

Maine
www.maine.gov/sos/cec/corp/

Maryland
www.dat.state.md.us/sdatweb/charter.html#newbiz

Massachusetts
www.sec.state.ma.us/cor/

Michigan
www.michigan.gov/cis/0,1607,7-154-35299_35413---,00.html

Appendix A

Minnesota
www.sos.state.mn.us/home/index.asp?page=3

Mississippi
www.sos.state.ms.us/busserv/corp/corporations.asp

Missouri
www.sos.mo.gov/business/corporations/

Montana
http://sos.mt.gov/BSB/index.asp

Nebraska
www.sos.state.ne.us/business/corp_serv/

Nevada
http://sos.state.nv.us/business/

New Hampshire
www.sos.nh.gov/corporate/

New Jersey
www.nj.gov/njbusiness/start/

New Mexico
www.nmprc.state.nm.us/cb.htm

New York
www.dos.state.ny.us/corp/corpwww.html

North Carolina
www.secretary.state.nc.us/corporations/thepage.aspx

North Dakota
www.nd.gov/sos/businessserv/

Ohio
www.sos.state.oh.us

Oklahoma
www.sos.state.ok.us/business/business_filing.htm

Oregon
www.filinginoregon.com

Pennsylvania
www.dos.state.pa.us/corps/site/default.asp

Rhode Island
www.sec.state.ri.us/corps/

South Carolina
www.scsos.com/corporations.htm

South Dakota
www.sdsos.gov/busineservices/corporations.shtm

Tennessee
www.state.tn.us/sos/bus_svc/corporations.htm

Texas
www.sos.state.tx.us/corp/index.shtml

Utah
http://corporations.utah.gov

Vermont
www.sec.state.vt.us/corps/corpindex.htm

Virginia
www.scc.virginia.gov/division/clk/diracc.htm

Washington
www.secstate.wa.gov/corps/

West Virginia
www.wvsos.com/business/main.htm

Wisconsin

www.wisconsin.gov/state/byb/corporation.html

Wyoming

http://soswy.state.wy.us/corporat/corporat.htm

Professional Reference Contacts

Author

Richard T. Williamson, Esq.
1945 Palo Verde Ave., Suite 101
Long Beach, CA 90815
Phone: 562-431-1956

Recommended Accountant

Matthew Crammer, EA
8141 E. 2nd St., Suite 340
Downey, CA 90241
Phone: 562-923-9436

Appendix B

(Example)
BYLAWS OF
RTW INVESTMENTS, INC
A CALIFORNIA CORPORATION

TABLE OF CONTENTS

ARTICLE I: OFFICES AND AGENTS
  Section 1. PRINCIPAL EXECUTIVE OFFICE
  Section 2. OTHER OFFICES
  Section 3. REGISTERED AGENTS

ARTICLE II: DIRECTORS—MANAGEMENT
  Section 1. RESPONSIBILITY OF BOARD OF DIRECTORS
  Section 2. NUMBER AND QUALIFICATION OF DIRECTORS
  Section 3. ELECTION, CUMULATIVE VOTING AND TERM OF OFFICE OF DIRECTORS
  Section 4. VACANCIES IN THE BOARD
  Section 5. REMOVAL OF DIRECTORS
  Section 6. COMPENSATION OF DIRECTORS
  Section 7. COMMITTEES OF THE BOARD
  Section 8. RESIGNATIONS OF A DIRECTOR
  Section 9. ADVISORY DIRECTORS
  Section 10. EXCEPTION FOR CLOSE CORPORATION

ARTICLE III: MEETINGS OF DIRECTORS
  Section 1. ANNUAL MEETINGS OF DIRECTORS
  Section 2. OTHER REGULAR MEETINGS OF DIRECTORS

Section 3. NOTICE OF ANNUAL AND OTHER REGULAR MEETINGS OF DIRECTORS
Section 4. SPECIAL MEETINGS OF DIRECTORS AND REQUIRED NOTICES
Section 5. NOTICE OF ADJOURNMENT OF MEETINGS
Section 6. WAIVER OR LACK OF NOTICE OF MEETING OF DIRECTORS
Section 7. DIRECTORS ACTION WITHOUT MEETING
Section 8. QUORUM FOR MEETINGS OF DIRECTORS
Section 9. EFFECT IF ONLY A SOLE DIRECTOR IS REQUIRED

ARTICLE IV: OFFICERS—MANAGEMENT
Section 1. OFFICERS
Section 2. ELECTION OF OFFICERS
Section 3. SUBORDINATE OFFICERS
Section 4. REMOVAL AND RESIGNATION OF OFFICERS
Section 5. VACANCIES IN AN OFFICE
Section 6. CHAIRMAN OF THE BOARD
Section 7. PRESIDENT
Section 8. VICE PRESIDENT
Section 9. SECRETARY
Section 10. CHIEF FINANCIAL OFFICER

ARTICLE V: MEETINGS OF SHAREHOLDERS
Section 1. PLACE OF MEETINGS
Section 2. ANNUAL MEETINGS OF SHAREHOLDERS
Section 3. SPECIAL MEETINGS OF SHAREHOLDERS
Section 4. LIST OF SHAREHOLDERS
Section 5. NOTICE OF MEETINGS OF SHAREHOLDERS
Section 6. WAIVER OF NOTICE OR CONSENT BY ABSENT SHAREHOLDERS
Section 7. SHAREHOLDERS ACTING WITHOUT A MEETING
Section 8. OTHER ACTIONS OF SHAREHOLDERS WITHOUT A MEETING
Section 9. QUORUM FOR MEETINGS OF SHAREHOLDERS
Section 10. VOTING BY SHAREHOLDERS
Section 11. FIXING DATE FOR MEETING OF SHAREHOLDERS
Section 12. PROXIES
Section 13. ORGANIZATION OF MEETINGS OF SHAREHOLDERS
Section 14. INSPECTORS OF ELECTION AT MEETINGS
Section 15. ELECTRONIC PARTICIPATION IN MEETINGS OF SHAREHOLDERS
Section 16. SHAREHOLDERS' AGREEMENTS

ARTICLE VI: CERTIFICATES AND TRANSFER OF SHARES
  Section 1. CERTIFICATES FOR SHARES
  Section 2. TRANSFER ON STOCK LEDGER
  Section 3. TRANSFER AGENTS AND REGISTRARS
  Section 4. RECORD DATE—CLOSING STOCK TRANSFER BOOKS
  Section 5. LEGEND CONDITION
  Section 6. LOST OR DESTROYED CERTIFICATES
  Section 7. CLOSE CORPORATION CERTIFICATES
  OPTIONAL:
  Section 8. PROVISION RESTRICTING TRANSFER OF SHARES AND FIRST REFUSAL RIGHTS
  Section 9. PLEDGED OR HYPOTHECATED SHARES

ARTICLE VII: RECORDS—INSPECTION-FILINGS-CHECKS-CONTRACTS—REPORTS
  Section 1. RECORDS
  Section 2. INSPECTION OF BOOKS AND RECORDS
  Section 3. ANNUAL FILINGS
  Section 4. CHECKS, DRAFTS, ETC.
  Section 5. EXECUTION OF CONTRACTS
  Section 6. WAIVER OF ANNUAL REPORT TO SHAREHOLDERS

ARTICLE VIII: AMENDMENTS TO BYLAWS AND CONSTRUCTION
  Section 1. AMENDMENT OF BYLAWS BY SHAREHOLDERS
  Section 2. AMENDMENT OF BYLAWS BY DIRECTORS
  Section 3. RECORD OF AMENDMENTS
  Section 4. CONSTRUCTION AND INTERPRETATION

ARTICLE IX: MISCELLANEOUS
  Section 1. CORPORATE SEAL
  Section 2. REPRESENTATION OF SHARES IN OTHERS
  Section 3. INDEMNIFICATION OF OFFICERS AND DIRECTORS
  Section 4. ACCOUNTING YEAR AND ACCOUNTING METHOD
  Section 5. OTHER TAX ELECTIONS
  Section 6. SUBSIDIARY CORPORATIONS
  Section 7. REFERENCES TO CODE SECTIONS

CERTIFICATE OF ADOPTION OF BYLAWS
  ADOPTION BY INCORPORATOR(S)
  CERTIFICATE BY SECRETARY
  CERTIFICATE BY SECRETARY OF ADOPTION BY SHAREHOLDERS' VOTE

BYLAWS
OF
RTW INVESTMENTS, INC

ARTICLE I
OFFICES AND AGENTS

Section 1. PRINCIPAL EXECUTIVE OFFICE. The principal executive office for the transaction of business of the corporation is hereby fixed and located at 1945 Palo Verde, Suite 101, City of Long Beach, County of Los Angeles, State of California.

The location of the principal executive office may be changed by approval of a majority of the authorized Directors, and additional offices may be established and maintained at such other place or places, either within or without the State of California, as the Board of Directors may from time to time designate.

Section 2. OTHER OFFICES. Branch or subordinate offices may at any time be established by the Board of Directors at any place or places where the corporation is qualified to do business.

Section 3. REGISTERED AGENTS. The corporation shall have and maintain a registered agent within the State of California and all within all other states in which it is required by applicable law.

ARTICLE II
DIRECTORS—MANAGEMENT

Section 1. RESPONSIBILITY OF BOARD OF DIRECTORS. Subject to the provisions of the corporation laws of the State of California (the "Corporation Law") and to any limitations in the Articles of Incorporation of the corporation relating to action required to be approved by the Shareholders, as that term is defined in Section 153 of the California Corporations Code, or by the outstanding shares, as that term is defined in Section 152 of the California Corporations Code, the business and affairs of the corporation shall be managed and all corporate powers shall be exercised by or under the direction of the Board of Directors. The Board may delegate the management of the day-to-day operation of the business of the corporation to a management company or other person, provided that the business and affairs of the corporation shall be managed and all corporate powers shall be exercised under the ultimate direction of the Board of Directors.

Each Director shall perform the duties of a Director, including the duties as a member of any committee of the Board upon which the Director may serve, in good faith, in a manner such Director believes to be in the best interests of the corporation, and with such care, including reasonable inquiry, as an ordinary prudent person in a like position would use under similar circumstances. (Sec. 309 of the California Corporations Code)

Section 2. NUMBER AND QUALIFICATION OF DIRECTORS. Subject to the Articles of Incorporation, the authorized Number of Directors shall be 1 [at least one if only one shareholder; at least two if two shareholders; at least three if three or more shareholders] until changed by a duly adopted amendment to the Articles of Incorporation if the number is fixed in the Articles of Incorporation or otherwise by an amendment to this bylaw adopted by the vote or written consent of holders of a majority of the outstanding shares entitled to vote. Each Director shall be a natural person of full age. A Director need not be a shareholder unless so required by the Articles of Incorporation. No reduction of the authorized number of Directors shall have the effect of removing any Director before that Director's term of office expires.

Section 3. ELECTION, CUMULATIVE VOTING, AND TERM OF OFFICE OF DIRECTORS. Subject to notice of cumulative voting and unless otherwise provided in the Articles of Incorporation, Directors shall be elected by the majority of the shares entitled to vote present, in person, or by proxy at each annual meeting of the Shareholders to hold office until the next annual meeting. Each Director, including a Director elected to fill a vacancy, shall hold office until the expiration of the term for which elected and until a successor has been elected and qualified or until such director's earlier resignation or removal.

Provided the name of the candidate has been placed in nomination prior to the voting and one or more Shareholder has given notice at the meeting prior to the voting of the Shareholder's intent to cumulate the Shareholder's votes, every Shareholder entitled to vote at any election for Directors of the corporation may cumulate their votes and give one candidate a number of votes equal to the number of Directors to be elected multiplied by the number of votes to which his or her shares are entitled, or distribute his or her votes on the same principle among as many candidates as he or she thinks fit. The candidates receiving the highest number of votes up to the number of Directors to be elected are elected.

Section 4. VACANCIES IN THE BOARD. A vacancy or vacancies in the Board of Directors shall be deemed to exist in the event of the death, resignation, or removal of any Director, or if the Board of Directors by resolution declares vacant the office of a Director who has been declared of unsound mind by an order of court or convicted of a felony, or if the authorized number of Directors is increased, or if the shareholders fail, at any meeting of shareholders at which any Director or Directors are elected, to elect the number of Directors to be voted for at that meeting.

Unless the Articles of Incorporation provide otherwise, vacancies in the Board of Directors may be filled A) by a majority vote of the remaining Directors at a meeting, or B) if the number of Directors is less than a quorum, by (1) unanimous written consent of the Directors then in office or (2) by the affirmative vote of a majority of the Directors then in office at a meeting.

If, after the filling of any vacancy by the Directors, the Directors then in office who have been elected by the Shareholders shall constitute less than a majority of the Directors then in office, then any holder or holders of an aggregate of 5 percent or more of the total number of shares at the time outstanding having the right to vote for those directors may call a special meeting of shareholders.

If the vacant office was held by a Director elected by a voting group of shareholders, only the holders of shares of that voting group are entitled to vote to fill the vacancy if it is filled by the shareholders. The shareholders may elect a Director to fill a vacancy not filled by the Directors by the written consent of the Shareholders holding a majority of the outstanding shares entitled to vote or by the vote of a majority of the shares entitled to vote represented at a duly held meeting at which a quorum is present. At any time, the

Shareholders may elect a Director or Directors to fill any vacancy or vacancies not filled by the Directors, but any such election by written consent shall require the consent of a majority of the outstanding shares entitled to vote.

Each Director so elected shall hold office until the next annual meeting of the Shareholders and until a successor has been elected and qualified.

Section 5. REMOVAL OF DIRECTORS. Except as otherwise provided in the Articles of Incorporation or the Corporation Law, the entire Board of Directors or any individual Director may be removed from office within or with or without cause by the holders of the shares then entitled to vote for the election of Directors, provided if a Director is elected by a voting group, only shareholders of the group may vote to remove and if less than the entire board is removed. A Director may not be removed if the number of votes sufficient to elect under cumulate voting votes against removal unless the entire Board is removed. A director may be removed by the shareholders only at a meeting called for the purpose of removing him and the meeting notice shall state that the purpose, or one (1) of the purposes, of the meeting is removal of the director. In such case, the remaining members of the Board may elect a successor Director to fill such vacancy for the remaining unexpired term of the Director so removed.

Section 6. COMPENSATION OF DIRECTORS. Directors, as such, shall not receive any stated salary for their services, but by resolution of the Board a fixed sum and expense of attendance, if any, may be allowed for attendance at each regular and special meeting of the Board; provided that nothing herein contained shall be construed to preclude any Director from serving the corporation in any other capacity and receiving compensation therefore.

Section 7.COMMITTEES OF THE BOARD. One or more Committees of the Board may be appointed by resolution passed by a majority of the authorized number of Directors of the Board. Committees shall be composed of one (1) or more members of the Board, and shall have such powers of the Board as may be expressly delegated to it by resolution of the Board of Directors, as permitted by the Corporation Law, except those powers expressly made non-delegable by Sec. 311.

The provisions of these Bylaws governing meetings of directors, notices of meeting, waiver of notice, quorum and voting shall apply to meetings of a committee. Any committee, to the extent provided in the resolution of the Board, shall have all the authority of the Board, except with respect to:

(a) the adoption, amendment, or the approval of any action for which the Corporation Law also requires shareholders' approval or approval of the outstanding shares;
(b) the creation or filling of vacancies on the Board of Directors or any committee of the Board;
(c) the fixing of compensation of the directors for serving on the Board or on any committee;
(d) the adoption, amendment or repeal of bylaws or the adoption of new bylaws;
(e) the amendment of the Articles of Incorporation;
(f) the amendment or repeal of any resolution of the Board of Directors which by its express terms is not so amendable or repealable;
(g) a distribution to the shareholders of the corporation, except at a rate or in a periodic amount or within a price range determined by the Board of Directors; or

(h) the appointment of any other committees of the Board of Directors or the members of these committees.

Section 8. RESIGNATIONS OF A DIRECTOR. Any Director may resign effective upon giving written notice to the Chairman of the Board, the President, the Board of Directors of the corporation or as otherwise allowed under the Corporation Law, unless the notice specifies a later time for the effectiveness of such resignation. If the resignation is effective at a future time, a successor may be elected to take office when the resignation becomes effective.

Section 9. ADVISORY DIRECTORS. The Board of Directors from time to time may elect one or more persons to be Advisory Directors who shall not by such appointment be members of the Board of Directors. Advisory Directors shall be available from time to time to perform special assignments specified by the President, to attend meetings of the Board of Directors upon invitation and to furnish consultation to the Board. The period during which the title shall be held may be prescribed by the Board of Directors. If no period is prescribed, the title shall be held at the pleasure of the Board.

Section 10. EXCEPTION FOR CLOSE CORPORATION. Notwithstanding the provisions of Section 1 of these Bylaws, in the event that this corporation shall elect to become a close corporation as defined in Sec. 158 of the California Corporations Code, its Shareholders may enter into a Shareholders' Agreement as defined in Sec. 186 of the California Corporations Code. Said Agreement may provide for the exercise of corporate powers and the management of the business and affairs of this corporation by the Shareholders, provided, however, such agreement shall, to the extent and so long as the discretion or the powers of the Board in its management of corporate affairs is controlled by such agreement, impose upon each Shareholder who is a party thereof, liability for managerial acts performed or omitted by such person pursuant thereto otherwise imposed upon Directors as provided in Sec. 300 (d) of the California Corporations Code; and the Directors shall be relieved to that extent from such liability.

ARTICLE III
MEETINGS OF DIRECTORS

Section 1. ANNUAL MEETINGS OF DIRECTORS. Meetings of the Board of Directors may be called by the Chairman of the Board, or the President, or any Vice President, or the Secretary, or any two (2) Directors and shall be held at the principal executive office of the corporation, unless some other place is designated in the notice of the meeting. Members of the Board may participate in a meeting through use of a conference telephone or similar communications equipment so long as all members participating in such a meeting can hear one another. Accurate minutes of any meeting of the Board or any committee thereof, shall be maintained by the Secretary or other officer designated for that purpose.

Section 2. OTHER REGULAR MEETINGS OF DIRECTORS. Regular meetings of the Board of Directors shall be held at the principal executive offices, or such other place as may be designated by the Board of Directors, as follows:

Time of Regular Meeting: 10:00 a.m.
Date of Regular Meeting: January 1

If said day shall fall upon a holiday, such meetings shall be held on the next succeeding business day thereafter.

Section 3. **NOTICE OF ANNUAL AND OTHER REGULAR MEETINGS OF DIRECTORS.** No notice need to be given of a regular (including annual) meeting of the Board of Directors if the time and place of the meeting is fixed by the bylaws or the Board of Directors. The notice of a regular (including annual) meeting need not specify the purpose of the meeting.

Section 4. **SPECIAL MEETINGS OF DIRECTORS AND REQUIRED NOTICES.** Special meetings of the Board may be called at any time by the Chairman of the Board or the President or any Vice President or the Secretary or any two (2) Directors. At least forty-eight (48) hours notice of the time, place and purpose of special meetings shall be delivered personally to the Directors or personally communicated to them by a corporate Officer by telephone or telegraph or by electronic transmission.

If the notice of a special meeting is sent to a Director by letter, it shall be addressed to him or her at his or her address as it is shown upon the records of the corporation, or if it is not so shown on such records or is not readily ascertainable, at the place in which the meetings of the Directors are regularly held. In case such notice is mailed, it shall be deposited in the United States mail, postage prepaid, in the place in which the principal executive office of the corporation is located at least four (4) days prior to the time of the holding of the meeting. The mailing, telegraphing, telephoning or delivery as above provided and any other method allowed by the Corporation Law shall be due, legal and personal notice to the Director.

Section 5. **NOTICE OF ADJOURNMENT OF MEETINGS.** A majority of the Directors present at a meeting, whether or not constituting a quorum, may adjourn the meeting to another time and place. Notice of the time and place of holding an adjourned meeting need not be given to absent Directors if the time and place be fixed at the meeting adjourned and held within any twenty-four (24) hours, but if adjourned more than twenty-four (24) hours, notice shall be given to all Directors not present at the time of the adjournment.

Section 6. **WAIVER OR LACK OF NOTICE OF MEETING OF DIRECTORS.** If there is any lack of required notice of any meeting of directors, then the transactions thereof are as valid as if had at a meeting regularly called and noticed provided all of the Directors are present at any Directors' meeting, however called or noticed, or all of the Directors not present sign a written consent to the holding of the meeting or approval of the minutes on the records of such meeting, before or after the time or date of meeting stated in the Notice. The waiver, consent or approval shall be filed with the Secretary of the corporation for filing with the minutes or corporate records. If a Director attends a meeting without notice but without protesting prior thereto or at its commencement, the Director shall be treated as present at the meeting.

Section 7. **DIRECTORS ACTION: WITHOUT MEETING.** Any action required or permitted to be taken by the Board of Directors may be taken without a meeting and with the same force and effect as if taken by a unanimous vote of Directors, if authorized by a writing signed individually or collectively by all members of the Board. Such consent reflecting the action taken shall be filed with the regular minutes of the Board.

Section 8. QUORUM FOR MEETINGS OF DIRECTORS. A majority of the total number of Directors shall be necessary to constitute a quorum for the transaction of business. Unless the Articles of Incorporation or Bylaws require a greater number, the action of a majority of the Directors present at any meeting at which there is a quorum, when duly assembled, is valid as a corporate act; provided that a minority of the Directors, in the absence of a quorum, may adjourn from time to time, but may not transact any business. A meeting at which a quorum is initially present may continue to transact business, notwithstanding the withdrawal of Directors, if any action taken is approved by a majority of the required quorum for such meeting.

Section 9. EFFECT IF ONLY A SOLE DIRECTOR IS REQUIRED. In the event only one (1) Director is required by the Bylaws or Articles of Incorporation, any reference herein to notices, waivers, consents, meetings or other actions by a majority or quorum of the Directors shall be deemed to refer to such notice, waiver, etc., by such sole Director, who shall have all the rights and duties and shall be entitled to exercise all of the powers and shall assume all the responsibilities otherwise herein described as given to a Board of Directors.

ARTICLE IV
OFFICERS—MANAGEMENT

Section 1. OFFICERS. The officers of the corporation shall be a President, a Secretary, and a Chief Financial Officer. The corporation may also have, at the discretion of the Board of Directors, a Chairman of the Board, one or more Vice Presidents, one or more Assistant Secretaries, one or more Assistant Treasurers, and such other Officers as may be appointed in accordance with the provisions of Section 3 of this Article III. Any number of offices may be held by the same person. Any two or more offices may be held simultaneously by the same person, except the offices of President and Secretary unless the Corporation has only one shareholder.

Section 2. ELECTION OF OFFICERS. The officers of the corporation, except such officers as may be appointed in accordance with the provisions of Section 3 relating to appointment of subordinate officers or Section 5 relating to vacancies of this Article, shall be chosen annually by the Board of Directors, and each shall hold office until he or she shall resign or shall be removed or otherwise disqualified to serve, or a successor shall be elected and qualified.

Section 3. SUBORDINATE OFFICERS. The Board of Directors may appoint such other officers as the business of the corporation may require, each of whom shall hold office for such period, have such authority and perform such duties as are provided in the Bylaws or as the Board of Directors may from time to time determine.

Section 4. REMOVAL AND RESIGNATION OF OFFICERS. Subject to the rights, if any, of an officer under any contract of employment, any officer may be removed, either with or without cause, by the Board of Directors, at any regular or special meeting to the Board. Any officer may resign at any time by giving written notice to the corporation. Any resignation shall take effect at the date of the receipt of that notice or at any later time specified in that notice; and, unless otherwise specified in that notice, the acceptance of the resignation shall not be necessary to make it effective. Any resignation is without prejudice to the rights, if any, of the corporation under any contract to which the officer is a party.

Section 5. VACANCIES IN AN OFFICE. A vacancy in any office because of death, resignation, removal, disqualification or any other cause shall be filled in the manner prescribed in the Bylaws for regular appointments to that office.

Section 6. CHAIRMAN OF THE BOARD. The Chairman of the Board, if such an officer be elected, shall, if present, preside at meetings of the Board of Directors and exercise and perform such other powers and duties as may be from time to time assigned by the Board of Directors or prescribed by the Bylaws. If there is no President, the Chairman of the Board shall in addition be the Chief Executive Officer of the corporation and shall have the powers and duties prescribed in Section 7 of this Article IV.

Section 7. PRESIDENT. Subject to such supervisory powers, if any, as may be given by the Board of Directors to the Chairman of the Board, if there be such an officer, the President shall be the Chief Executive Officer of the corporation and shall, subject to the control of the Board of Directors, have general supervision, direction and control of the business and officers of the corporation. He or she shall preside at all meetings of the Shareholders and in the absence of the Chairman of the Board, or if there be none, at all meetings of the Board of Directors. The President shall be ex officio a member of all the standing committees, including the Executive Committee, if any, and shall have the general powers and duties of management usually vested in the office of President of a corporation, and shall have such other powers and duties as may be prescribed by the Board of Directors or the Bylaws.

Section 8. VICE PRESIDENT. In the absence or disability of the President, the Vice Presidents, if any, in order of their rank as fixed by the Board of Directors, or if not ranked, the Vice President designated by the Board of Directors, shall perform all the duties of the President, and when so acting shall have all the powers of, and be subject to, all the restrictions upon, the President. The Vice Presidents shall have such other powers and perform such other duties as from time to time may be prescribed for them respectively by the Board of Directors or the Bylaws.

Section 9. SECRETARY. The Secretary shall have the following duties:

(A) *Book of Minutes.* The Secretary shall keep, or cause to be kept, a book of minutes at the principal office or such other place as the Board of Directors may order, of all meetings of Directors and Shareholders, with the time and place of holding, whether regular or special, and if special, how authorized, the notice thereof given, the names of those present at Directors' meetings, the number of shares present or represented at Shareholders' meetings and the proceedings thereof.

(B) *Record of Shareholders.* The Secretary shall keep, or cause to be kept, at the principal office or at the office of the corporation's transfer agent, a share register, or duplicate share register, showing the names of the Shareholders and their addresses; the number and classes of shares held by each; the number and date of certificates issued for the same; and the number and date of cancellation of every certificate surrendered for cancellation.

(C) *Notice of Meetings.* The Secretary shall give, or cause to be given, notice of all the meetings of the Shareholders and of the Board of Directors required by the Bylaws or by law to be given. He or she shall keep the seal of the corporation in safe custody, and shall have such other powers and perform such other duties as may be prescribed by the Board of Directors or by the Bylaws.

(D) *Other Duties.* The Secretary shall keep the seal of the corporation, if any, in safe custody. The Secretary shall have such other powers and perform such other duties as prescribed by the bylaws or by the Board of Directors.

Section 10. CHIEF FINANCIAL OFFICER. The Chief Financial Officer shall keep and maintain, or cause to be kept and maintained in accordance with generally accepted accounting principles, adequate and correct accounts of the properties and business transactions of the corporation, including accounts of its assets, liabilities, receipts, disbursements, gains, losses, capital, earnings (or surplus) and shares. The books of account shall at all reasonable times be open to inspection by any Director.

The Chief Financial Officer shall deposit all moneys and other valuables in the name and to the credit of the corporation with such depositaries as may be designated by the Board of Directors. He or she shall disburse the funds of the corporation as may be ordered by the Board of Directors, shall render to the President and Directors, whenever they request it, an account of all of his or her transactions and of the financial condition of the corporation, and shall have such other powers and perform such other duties as may be prescribed by the Board of Directors or the Bylaws.

ARTICLE V
MEETINGS OF SHAREHOLDERS

Section 1. PLACE OF MEETINGS. Unless otherwise provided in the Articles of Incorporation, all meetings of the Shareholders shall be held at the principal executive office of the corporation within the State of California unless some other appropriate and convenient geographical location is designated for that purpose from time to time by a resolution of the Board of Directors.

Section 2. ANNUAL MEETINGS OF SHAREHOLDERS. The annual meetings of the Shareholders shall be held, each year, at the time and on the day and location following:

Time of Annual Meeting:
Date of Annual Meeting:
Location of Annual Meeting:

If this day shall be a legal holiday, then the meeting shall be held on the next succeeding business day, at the same hour. At the annual meeting, the Shareholders shall elect a Board of Directors, consider reports of the affairs of the corporation and transact such other business as may be properly brought before the meeting. The initial annual meeting of Shareholders shall be held within fifteen (15) months of the date of the filing of the Articles of Incorporation with the Secretary of State.

Section 3. SPECIAL MEETINGS OF SHAREHOLDERS. Special meetings of the Shareholders may be called at any time by the Board of Directors, Chairman of the Board of Directors, the President, or by one or more Shareholders holding not less than one-tenth (1/10) of the votes entitled to be cast on any issue proposed to be considered at the special meeting.

Upon receipt of a written request addressed to the Chairman, President, Vice President, or Secretary, mailed or delivered personally to such officer by any person (other than the Board) entitled to call a special meeting of Shareholders, such officer shall cause notice to be given to the Shareholders entitled to vote, and a meeting will be held at a time requested by the person or persons calling the meeting, not less than thirty-five (35) nor more than sixty (60) days after the receipt of such request. If such notice is not given within twenty (20) days after receipt of such request, the persons calling the meeting may give notice thereof in the manner provided by these Bylaws or apply to the Superior Court as provided in Sec. 305(c)(2) of the California Corporations Code.

Section 4. LIST OF SHAREHOLDERS. After the record date for a meeting has been fixed, the corporation shall prepare an alphabetized list of names, addresses and number of shares of all shareholders, entitled to notice, arranged by voting group, and within each voting group by class or series in each case as reflected in the recasts of the Corporation.

The list shall be available for inspection by any shareholder beginning two days after the notice of the meeting is given.

Section 5. NOTICE OF MEETINGS OF SHAREHOLDERS. of meetings, annual or special, shall be given in writing not less than ten (10) nor more than sixty (60) days before the-date of the meeting to Shareholders entitled to vote thereat. The notices shall be given by the Secretary or the Assistant Secretary, or if there be no such officer, or in the case of his or her neglect or refusal, by any Director or Shareholder.

The notices shall be given personally or by mail or other means of written communication allowed under the Corporation Law including by personal delivery, first class mail, facsimile, E-mail, or other form of electronic transmission and shall be sent to the Shareholder's address appearing on the books of the corporation, or supplied by him or her to the corporation for the purpose of notice, and in the absence thereof, as provided under the Corporation Law.

Notice of any meeting of Shareholders shall specify the place, the day and the hour of meeting, the means, if any, of electronic or remote participation by which a shareholder may participate and be considered present and eligible to vote, and (1) in case of a special meeting, the general nature of the business to be transacted and no other business may be transacted, or (2) in the case of an annual meeting, those matters which the Board at date of mailing, intends to present for action by the Shareholders. At any meetings where Directors are to be elected, notice shall include the names of the nominees, if any, intended at date of notice to be presented by management for election.

The notice shall also state the general nature of any proposed action to be taken at the meeting to approve any of the following matters: (i) a contract or transaction in which a director has a direct or indirect financial interest, pursuant to Section 310 of the California Corporations Code; (ii) an amendment to the Articles of Incorporation under Section 902 of the California Corporations Code; (iii) a reorganization under Section 1201 of the California Corporations Code; (iv) a voluntary dissolution of the corporation under Section 1900 of the California Corporations Code; or (v) a distribution in dissolution other than in accordance with the rights of outstanding preferred shares, pursuant to Section 2007 of the California Corporations Code. If a Shareholder supplies no address, notice shall be deemed to have been given if mailed to the place where the principal executive office of the corporation, in California, is situated, or published at least once in some newspaper of general circulation in the County of said principal office.

Notice shall be deemed given at the time it is delivered personally or deposited in the mail or sent by other means of written communication. The officer giving such notice or report shall prepare and file an affidavit or declaration thereof.

When a meeting is adjourned for forty-five (45) days or more, notice of the adjourned meeting shall be given as in case of an original meeting. Save, as aforesaid, it shall not be necessary to give any notice of adjournment or of the business to be transacted at an adjourned meeting other than by announcement at the meeting at which such adjournment is taken.

Section 6. WAIVER OF NOTICE OR CONSENT BY ABSENT SHAREHOLDERS. A shareholder may in writing waiver any notice of meeting before or after the date of meeting stated in the notice, as allowed under Sec. 601 (e) of the California Corporations Code.

Section 7. SHAREHOLDERS ACTING WITHOUT A MEETING. Unless otherwise provided in the Articles of Incorporation, any action which may be taken at a meeting of the Shareholders, may be taken without a meeting or notice of meeting if authorized by a writing signed by all of the Shareholders entitled to vote at a meeting for such purpose, setting forth the action taken and filed with the Secretary of the corporation for filing with the minutes of proceedings of the Board in the records of the corporation.

While ordinarily Directors can only be elected by unanimous written consent of the shareholders, if the Directors fail to fill a vacancy, then a Director to fill that vacancy may be elected by the written consent of persons holding a majority of shares entitled to vote for the election of Directors.

If the consents of all Shareholders entitled to vote have not been solicited in writing, and if the unanimous written consent of all Shareholders shall not have been received, the Secretary shall give prompt notice of the corporate action approved by the shareholders without a meeting. This notice shall be given in the manner specified in Section 2.5 of this ARTICLE II. In the case of approval of (i) contracts or transactions in which a director has a direct or indirect financial interest, pursuant to Section 310 of the California Corporations Code of California, (ii) indemnification of agents of the corporation, pursuant to Section 317 of that Code, (iii) a reorganization of the corporation, pursuant to Section 1201 of the California Corporations Code, and (iv) a distribution in dissolution other than in accordance with the rights of outstanding preferred shares, pursuant to Section 2007 of the California Corporations Code, the notice shall be given at least ten (10) days before the consummation of any action authorized by that approval.

Section 8. OTHER ACTIONS OF SHAREHOLDERS WITHOUT A MEETING. Unless otherwise provided in the Corporations Law or the Articles of Incorporation, any action which may be taken at any annual or special meeting of Shareholders may be taken without a meeting and without prior notice, if a consent in writing, setting forth the action so taken, signed and dated by the holders of outstanding shares having not less than the minimum number of votes that would be necessary to authorized or take such action at a meeting at which all shares entitled to vote thereon were present and voted. The signed action shall be delivered to the corporation as required by the Corporation Law.

Unless the consents of all Shareholders entitled to vote have been solicited in writing, notice of any approval by Shareholders without a meeting by less than unanimous written consent shall be given at least ten (10) days before the consummation of the action authorized by such approval, and prompt notice shall be given of the taking of any other corporate action approved by Shareholders without a meeting by less than unanimous written consent, to each of those Shareholders entitled to vote who have not consented in writing.

Any Shareholder giving a written consent, or the proxyholder of the Shareholder, or a transferee of the shares of a personal representative of the Shareholder or their respective proxyholders, may revoke the consent by a writing received by the corporation prior to the time that written consents of the number of shares required to authorize the proposed action have been filed with the Secretary of the corporation, but may not do so thereafter. Such revocation is effective upon its receipt by the Secretary of the corporation.

Section 9. QUORUM FOR MEETINGS OF SHAREHOLDERS. The holders of a majority of the shares entitled to vote thereat, that are present in person, or by use of authorized communications equipment or represented by proxy shall constitute a quorum at all meetings of the Shareholders for the transaction of business except as otherwise provided by these Bylaws. If, however, such majority (or other required greater number) shall not be present or represented at any meeting of the Shareholders, the Shareholders entitled to vote thereat, present in person, or by proxy, shall have the power to adjourn the meeting from time to time, until the requisite amount of voting shares shall be present. At such adjourned meeting at which the requisite amount of voting shares shall be represented, any business may be transacted which might have been transacted at a meeting as originally notified.

If a quorum be initially present, the Shareholders may continue to transact business for the remainder of the meeting until adjournment, notwithstanding the withdrawal of enough Shareholders to leave less than a quorum, if any action taken is approved by a majority of the Shareholders required to initially constitute a quorum.

Section 10. VOTING BY SHAREHOLDERS. Unless otherwise provided in the Articles of Incorporation or the Corporation Law, each shareholder of record on the day next mentioned shall be entitled to one vote for each share of stock held. The shareholders may vote by voice or ballot provided their own election for directors must be by voice only if demanded by any shareholder before the voting has begun. Only persons in whose names shares entitled to vote stand on the stock records of the corporation on the day of any meeting of Shareholders, unless some other day be fixed by the Board of Directors for the determination of Shareholders of record, and then on such other day, shall be entitled to vote at such meeting.

Section 11. FIXING DATE FOR MEETINGS OF SHAREHOLDERS. The Board of Directors may fix a time in the future not exceeding sixty (60) days preceding the date of any meeting of Shareholders or less than ten (10) days, as a record date for the determination of the Shareholders entitled to notice of and to vote at any such meeting. In such case only Shareholders of record on the date so fixed shall be entitled to notice of and to vote at such meeting, as the case may be notwithstanding any transfer of any share on the books of the corporation after any record date fixed as aforesaid. The Board of Directors may close the books of the corporation against transfers of shares during the whole or any part of such period.

Section 12. PROXIES. Every Shareholder entitled to vote, or to execute consents, may do so, either in person or by written proxy or otherwise executed and transmitted to the Corporation in accordance with the provisions of the Corporation Law. A proxy is valid for a maximum period provided in the Corporation Law (Secs. 604 and 705 of the California Corporations Code) unless revoked or a different period is stated therein.

Every person entitled to vote for directors or on any other matter shall have the right to do so either in person or by one or more agents authorized by a written proxy signed by the person and filed with the Secretary of the corporation. A proxy shall be deemed signed if the shareholder's name is placed on the proxy (whether by manual signature, typewriting, telegraphic transmission, or otherwise) by the shareholder or the shareholder's attorney in fact. A validly executed proxy which does not state that it is irrevocable shall continue in full force and effect unless (i) revoked by the person executing it, before the vote pursuant to that proxy, by a writing delivered to the corporation stating that the proxy is revoked, or by a subsequent proxy executed by, or attendance at the meeting and voting in person by, the person executing the proxy; or (ii) written notice of the death or incapacity of the maker of that proxy is received by the corporation before the vote pursuant to that proxy is counted; provided, however, that no proxy shall be valid after the expiration of eleven (11) months from the date of the proxy, unless otherwise provided in the proxy. The revocability of a proxy that states on its face that it is irrevocable shall be governed by the provisions of Sections 705(e) and 705(f) of the California Corporations Code.

Section 13. ORGANIZATION OF MEETINGS OF SHAREHOLDERS. The President, or in the absence of the President, any Vice President, shall call the meeting of the Shareholders to order, and shall act as chairman of the meeting. In the absence of the President and all of the Vice Presidents, Shareholders shall appoint a chairman for such meeting. The Secretary of the corporation shall act as Secretary of all meetings of the Shareholders, but in the absence of the Secretary at any meeting of the Shareholders, the presiding officer may appoint any person to act as Secretary of the meeting.

Section 14. INSPECTORS OF ELECTION AT MEETINGS. In advance of any meeting of Shareholders, the Board of Directors may, if they so appoint inspectors of election to act at such meeting or any adjournment thereof. If inspectors of election be not so appointed, or if any persons so appointed fail to appear or refuse to act, the chairman of any such meeting may, and on the request of any Shareholder or his or her proxy] shall, make such appointment at the meeting in which case the number of inspectors shall be either one (1) or three (3) as determined by a majority of the Shareholders represented at the meeting.

These inspectors shall:

(a) determine the number of shares outstanding and the voting power of each share;
(b) determine the shares represented at the meeting and the existence of a quorum;
(c) determine the authenticity, validity, and effect of proxies and ballots;
(d) receive votes, ballots, waivers, releases, or consents;
(e) hear and determine all challenges and questions in any way arising in connection with the right to vote or the vote;
(f) count and tabulate all votes or consents;

(g) determine when the polls shall close;
(h) determine the result; and
(i) do any other acts that may be proper to conduct the election or vote with fairness to all shareholders.

Section 15. ELECTRONIC PARTICIPATION IN MEETINGS OF SHAREHOLDERS. If authorized by the Board of Directors in its sole discretion and subject to any guidelines or procedures adopted by the Board of Directors and subject to consent described in Section 20 Shareholders and proxyholders may participate in a meeting of shareholders by means of a telephone conference or any similar method of electronic communication or transmission by which all persons participating in the meeting can hear and speak to each other. Participation by such means constitutes presence in person at the meeting.

A meeting of shareholders may be conducted, in whole or in part, by electronic transmission by and to the corporation or by electronic video screen communication (1) if the corporation implements reasonable measures to provide shareholders (in person or by proxy) a reasonable opportunity to participate in the meeting and to vote on matters submitted to the shareholders, including an opportunity to read or hear the proceedings of the meeting concurrently with those proceedings, and (2) if any shareholder votes or takes other action at the meeting by means of electronic transmission to the Corporation or electronic video screen communication, a record of that vote or action is maintained by the corporation. Any request by a corporation to a shareholder pursuant to clause (b) of Section 20 of the California Corporations Code for consent to conduct a meeting of shareholders by electronic transmission by and to the Corporation, shall include a notice that absent consent of the shareholder pursuant to clause (b) of Section 20 of the California Corporations Code, the meeting shall be held at a physical location in accordance with subdivision (a).

Section 16. (A) SHAREHOLDERS' AGREEMENTS. Notwithstanding the above provisions, in the event the corporation elects to become a close corporation, an agreement between two (2) or more Shareholders thereof, if in writing and signed by the parties thereof, may provide that in exercising any voting rights the shares held by them shall be voted as provided therein or in Sec. 706 of the California Corporations Code, and may otherwise modify these provisions as to Shareholders' meetings and actions.

(B) EFFECT OF SHAREHOLDERS' AGREEMENTS. Any Shareholders' Agreement authorized by Sec. 300 (b) of the California Corporations Code, shall only be effective to modify the terms of these Bylaws if this corporation elects to become a close corporation with appropriate filing of or amendment to its Articles as required by Section 202 of the California Corporations Code and shall terminate when this corporation ceases to be a close corporation. Such an agreement cannot waive or alter Section 158, (defining close corporations), Section 202 (requirements of Articles of Incorporation), Section 500 and Section 501 relative to distributions, Section 111 (merger), Section 1201 (e) (reorganization) or Chapters 15 (Records and Reports) or Section 16 (Rights of Inspection), Section 18 (Involuntary Dissolution) or Section 22 (Crimes and Penalties), all of the California Corporations Code. Any other provisions of the Code or these Bylaws may be altered or waived thereby, but to the extent they are not so altered or waived, these Bylaws shall be applicable.

ARTICLE VI
CERTIFICATES AND TRANSFER OF SHARES

Section 1. CERTIFICATES FOR SHARES. Certificates for shares shall be of such form and device as the Board of Directors may designate and shall state on the face the name of the corporation, state of incorporation, the name of the record holder of the shares represented thereby; the number of shares represented, class of shares, designation of series; par value of the shares or a statement that the shares are without par value; date of issuance; a statement of the rights, privileges, preferences, restrictions or limitations, if any; with reference to the provisions of the Articles of Incorporation and any actions of the Directors establishing same. A conspicuous statement as to the rights of redemption or conversion, if any; a statement of liens or restrictions upon transfer or voting, if any; whether or not the shares are assessable or, whether assessments are collectible by personal action and any other express terms and the authority of the Board of Directors to determine variation for future series.

All certificates representing shares of the corporation if it elects to be a close corporation shall contain in addition to any other statements required, the following conspicuous legend on the face thereof:

"This Corporation is a close corporation. The number of holders of record of its shares of all classes cannot exceed. Any attempted voluntary inter vivos transfer which would violate this requirement is void. Refer to the Articles, Bylaws, and any agreements on file with the secretary of the Corporation for further restrictions."

All certificates shall be signed in the name of the corporation by the Chairman of the Board or Vice Chairman of the Board or the President or Vice President and by the Secretary or Chief Financial Officer certifying the number of shares and the class or series of shares owned by the Shareholder.

Any or all of the signatures on the certificate may be facsimile. In case any officer, transfer agent, or registrar who has signed or whose facsimile signature has been placed on a certificate shall have ceased to be that officer, transfer agent, or registrar before that certificate is issued, it may be issued by the corporation with the same effect as if that person were an officer, transfer agent, or registrar at the date of issue.

Section 2. TRANSFER ON STOCK LEDGER. Upon surrender to the Secretary or transfer agent of the corporation of a certificate for shares duly endorsed or accompanied by proper evidence of succession, assignment or authority to transfer, it shall be the duty of the corporation to issue a new certificate to the person entitled thereto, cancel the old certificate and record the transaction upon its stock ledger.

Section 3. TRANSFER AGENTS AND REGISTRARS. The Board of Directors may appoint one or more transfer agents or transfer clerks, and one or more registrars, which shall be an incorporated bank or trust company, either domestic or foreign, who, shall be appointed at such times and places as the requirements of the corporation may necessitate and the Board of Directors may designate.

Section 4. RECORD DATE—CLOSING STOCK TRANSFER BOOKS. In order that the corporation may determine the Shareholders entitled to notice of any meeting or to vote or entitled to receive payment of any dividend or other distribution or allotment of any rights or entitled to exercise any rights in respect of any other lawful action, the Board may fix, in advance, a record date, which shall not be more than sixty (60) nor less than ten (10) days prior to the date of such meeting nor more than sixty (60) days.

If no record date is fixed; the record date for determining Shareholders entitled to notice of or to vote at a meeting of Shareholders shall be at the close of business on the business day next preceding the day on which notice is given, or, if notice is waived, at the close of business on the business day next preceding the day on which the meeting is held.

Unless the Articles of Incorporation or the Corporation Law provide otherwise, the record date for determining Shareholders entitled to give consent to corporate action in writing without a meeting, when no prior action by the Board of Directors is necessary, shall be the day on which the first written consent is given by delivery to the registered office of the corporation in the State of California.

Unless the Articles of Incorporation or the Corporation Law otherwise provides, the record date for determining Shareholders for any other purpose shall be at the close of business on the day on which the Board adopts the resolution relating thereto, or the sixtieth (60th) day, prior to the date of such other action, whichever is later.

Section 5. LEGEND CONDITION. In the event any shares of this corporation are issued pursuant to a permit or exemption therefrom requiring the imposition of a legend condition, the person or persons issuing or transferring said shares shall make sure said legend appears on the certificate and shall not be required to transfer any shares free of such legend unless an amendment to such permit or a new permit be first issued so authorizing such a deletion.

Section 6. LOST OR DESTROYED CERTIFICATES. Any person claiming a certificate of stock to be lost or destroyed shall make an affidavit or affirmation of the fact and shall, if the Directors so require, give the corporation a bond of indemnity, in form and with one or more sureties satisfactory to the Board, in at least double the value of the stock represented by said certificate, whereupon a new certificate may be issued in the same tenor and for the same number of shares as the one alleged to be lost or destroyed.

Section 7. CLOSE CORPORATION CERTIFICATES. All certificates representing shares of this corporation, in the event it shall elect to become a close corporation, shall contain the legend required by Sec. 418 (c) of the California Corporations Code.

ARTICLE VII
RECORDS—INSPECTION - FILINGS - CHECKS - CONTRACTS - REPORTS

Section 1. RECORDS. The corporation shall maintain, in accordance with generally accepted accounting principles, adequate, appropriate, complete and correct accounts, books and records of its business and properties. The corporation shall maintain a copy of the Articles of Incorporation certified as filed by the Secretary of State and all amendments thereto, minutes of proceedings or consents of incorporators, a copy of the Bylaws certified by an officer of the corporation and all amendments thereto, resolutions adopted by the Board of Directors including but not limited to those creating one or more classes or series of shares and fixed relative rights, preferences and limitations, minutes of all meetings of shareholders, all written communications by Corporation to Shareholders, a stock ledger reflecting the original issuance of shares, revised at least annually and a current list of its shareholders showing number of shares of each class and series held and address of each shareholder names alphabetically arranged by voting group and within each voting group by class or series, names and addresses of current directors and officers, annual report most recently filed with the Secretary of State, financial statements for the past three years and tax returns for the past six years. All of such books, records, accounts, documents, ledgers and lists shall be kept at its principal executive office in the State of California, as fixed by the Board of Directors from time to time. The above mentioned records or a copy thereof shall remain at the principal office of the Corporation.

Section 2. INSPECTION OF BOOKS AND RECORDS. The Corporation shall keep at its principal executive office in this state, or if its principal executive office is not in California, at its principal business office in this state, the original or a copy of its Bylaws as amended to date, which shall be open to inspection by any Shareholder at all reasonable times during office hours. If the principal executive office of the corporation is outside California at the corporation has no principal business office in this state, it shall upon the written request of any Shareholder furnish to such Shareholder a copy of the Bylaws.

The accounting books and records and minutes of proceedings of the Shareholders and the Board and committees of the board of the corporation shall be open to inspection upon the written demand on the corporation of any Shareholder or holder of a voting trust certificate at any reasonable time during usual business hours, for a purpose reasonably related to such holder's interests as a Shareholder or as the holder of such voting certificate. The right of inspection shall extend to the records of each subsidiary of a corporation subject to this subdivision. Such inspection by a Shareholder or holder of a voting trust certificate may be made in person or by agent or attorney, and the right of inspection includes the right to copy and make extracts. The right of the Shareholders to inspect the corporate records may not be limited by the Articles or Bylaws.

Every Director shall have the absolute right at any reasonable time to inspect and copy all books, records, and documents of every kind and to inspect the physical properties of the corporation of which such person is a Director and also of its subsidiary corporations, domestic or foreign. Such inspection by a director may be made in person or by agent or attorney and the right of inspection includes the right to copy and make extracts.

Section 3. ANNUAL FILINGS. As required by the Corporation Law, the corporation shall periodically file a statement or list with the Secretary of State with any fees required.

Section 4. CHECKS, DRAFTS, ETC. All checks, drafts, or other orders for payment of money, notes or other evidences of indebtedness, issued in the name of or payable to the corporation, shall be signed or endorsed by such person or persons and in such manner as shall be determined from time to time by resolution of the Board of Directors.

Section 5. EXECUTION OF CONTRACTS. The Board of Directors, except as in the Bylaws otherwise provided, may authorize any officer or officers, agent or agents, to enter into any contract or execute any instrument in the name of and on behalf of the corporation. Such authority may be general or confined to specific instances. Unless so authorized by the Board of Directors, no officer, agent or employee shall have any power or authority to bind the corporation by any contract or agreement, or to pledge its credit, or to render it liable for any purpose or to any amount, except as provided in Sec. 313 of the Corporations Code.

Section 6. WAIVER OF ANNUAL REPORT TO SHAREHOLDERS. The annual report to Shareholders is expressly dispensed with so long as this corporation shall have less than one hundred (100) Shareholders. However, nothing herein shall be interpreted as prohibiting the Board of Directors from issuing annual or other periodic reports to the Shareholders of the corporation as they consider appropriate.

ARTICLE VIII
AMENDMENTS TO BYLAWS AND CONSTRUCTION

Section 1. AMENDMENT OF BYLAWS BY SHAREHOLDERS. Subject to the Corporation Law or the Articles of Incorporation, replacement Bylaws may be adopted or these Bylaws may be amended or repealed by the vote or written consent of holders of a majority of the outstanding shares entitled to vote; provided, however, that if the Articles of Incorporation of the corporation set forth the number of authorized Directors of the corporation, the authorized number of Directors may be changed only by an amendment of the Articles of Incorporation.

After the issuance of shares, a Bylaw specifying or changing a fixed number of directors or the maximum number or changing from a fixed to a variable number may be adopted by approval of a majority of the outstanding shares. An amendment of the Bylaws to reduce the fixed or minimum number to less than five cannot be adopted if votes cast against the adoption (or not consenting) are more than 16 2/3 percent of the outstanding shares entitled to vote

Section 2. AMENDMENT OF BYLAWS BY DIRECTORS. The Board of Directors may adopt, amend or repeal any of these Bylaws other than a Bylaw or amendment thereto fixing the authorized number of Directors or changing a quorum or voting requirement for the Board of Directors provided the power to amend the Bylaws is conferred or permitted in the Articles of Incorporation.

Section 3. RECORD OF AMENDMENTS. Whenever an amendment or new Bylaw is adopted, it shall be copied in the book of Bylaws with the original Bylaws, in the appropriate place. If any Bylaw is repealed, the fact of repeal with the date of the meeting at which the repeal was enacted or written assent was filed shall be stated in the book of Bylaws.

Section 4. CONSTRUCTION AND INTERPRETATION. Unless the context requires otherwise, the general provision rules of construction and definition of the Corporation Law shall govern the Bylaws. Without limiting the generality of this provision, the singular number includes plural, the plural number includes the singular. These Bylaws (and any amendments thereto) shall not be construed in a manner inconsistent with the Articles of Incorporation or the applicable provisions of the Corporation Law. Any provision of the Bylaws that is inconsistent with the Articles of Incorporation or Corporation Law shall be invalid only to the extent reasonably necessary for the provision to comply with the Articles of Incorporation or Corporation Law as the case may be.

ARTICLE IX
MISCELLANEOUS

Section 1. CORPORATE SEAL. The corporate seal shall be circular in form, and shall have inscribed thereon the name of the corporation, the year or date of its incorporation, and the state of incorporation.

Section 2. REPRESENTATION OF SHARES IN OTHERS. Shares of other corporations standing in the name of this corporation may be voted or represented and all incidents thereto may be exercised on behalf of the corporation by the Chairman of the Board, the President or any Vice President and the Secretary or an Assistant Secretary.

Section 3. INDEMNIFICATION OF OFFICERS AND DIRECTORS. The liability of the officers and directors of the corporation for monetary damages shall be eliminated to the fullest extent permissible under the Corporation Law. The corporation may provide and maintain insurance on behalf of any person serving as director or other officer against any liability asserted against such person.

Section 4. ACCOUNTING YEAR AND ACCOUNTING METHOD. The accounting year and accounting method of the corporation shall be fixed by resolution of the Board of Directors.

Section 5. OTHER TAX ELECTIONS. The Board of Directors may authorize the Chief Financial Officer to prepare and file such other tax elections as the Board of Directors deems appropriate.

Section 6. SUBSIDIARY CORPORATIONS. Shares of this corporation owned by a subsidiary shall not be entitled to vote on any matter. A subsidiary for these purposes is defined as a corporation, the shares of which possessing more than 25% of the total combined voting power of all classes of shares entitled to vote, are owned directly or indirectly through one (1) or more subsidiaries.

Section 7. REFERENCES TO CODE SECTIONS. "Sec." references herein refer to the equivalent Sections of the California Corporations Code effective January 1, 1977, as amended. The corporation is authorized to provide indemnification of agents as defined in [Section 317 of the California Corporations Code] for breach of duty to the corporation and shareholders through bylaw provisions or through agreements with the agents, or both, in excess of the indemnification otherwise permitted by [Section 317 of the California Corporations Code], subject to the limits on such excess indemnification set forth in [Section 204 of the California Corporations Code].

CERTIFICATE OF ADOPTION OF BYLAWS
OF
RTW INVESTMENTS, INC

ADOPTION BY FIRST DIRECTOR(S).

The undersigned Director(s) named in the Articles of Incorporation, or the duly elected First Director(s) of the above named corporation, hereby adopt the same as the Bylaws of said corporation.

Executed on: January 1

_____

Ralph Thomas Willis, Director

CERTIFICATE OF SECRETARY
OF
RTW INVESTMENTS, INC

I DO HEREBY CERTIFY AS FOLLOWS:

That I am the duly elected, qualified and acting Secretary of the above named corporation, that the foregoing Bylaws were adopted as the Bylaws of said corporation on the date set forth above by the person(s) named in the Articles of Incorporation as the Incorporator(s) or First Director(s) of said corporation.

IN WITNESS WHEREOF, I have hereunto set my hand and affixed the corporate seal on January 1.

_____

Ralph Thomas Willis, Secretary

Appendix C

(Example)

MINUTES OF ORGANIZATIONAL MEETING OF DIRECTORS OF RTW INVESTMENTS, INC A CALIFORNIA CORPORATION

Initial Directors of the Corporation appointed in the Articles of Incorporation filed with the Secretary of State or appointed by the Incorporator(s) pursuant to an action taken by unanimous consent held the organizational meeting of the initial Directors of the Corporation at the following date, time and place:

Date: January 1
Time: 10:00 a.m.
Place: 1945 Palo Verde Ave #101

The following persons were present and accepted their appointment as Directors:

Ralph Thomas Willis

The following persons officiated at the meeting:

Chair of meeting: Ralph Thomas Willis
Secretary of meeting: Ralph Thomas Willis

The chair called the meeting to order and announced that the meeting was held pursuant to written waivers of notice and consents to the holding of the meeting. The waivers and consents were presented to the meeting and, on a motion duly made, seconded, and carried, were made a part of the records and ordered inserted in the Record Book of Corporation immediately preceding the minutes of this meeting.

1. ARTICLES OF INCORPORATION

The chair informed the Directors present that the original Articles of Incorporation had been filed in the Office of the Secretary of State on January 1, 2009. A certified copy of the Articles of Incorporation has been provided to the secretary, and the secretary is hereby directed to insert the copy in the Record Book of the Corporation. A copy is attached as Exhibit "A." The following resolution was moved, seconded and adopted:

RESOLVED, that the Secretary is instructed to insert a copy of the Articles of Incorporation of the Corporation, certified by the Secretary of State, in the Record Book of the Corporation.

2. RESOLUTION OR ACTION OF INCORPORATOR(S)

The chair presented the resolution or action of Incorporators and their resignations. A copy is attached as Exhibit A-1. The following resolution was moved, seconded, and adopted:

RESOLVED, that the Secretary is instructed to insert the resolution or action of Incorporators and the resignation of Incorporators in the Record Book of the Corporation.

3. BYLAWS

The chair presented the Bylaws attached to these Minutes as Exhibit "B." The following resolutions were moved, seconded and adopted:

RESOLVED, that the Bylaws attached to these Minutes as Exhibit "B" are adopted as the Bylaws of the Corporation; and

RESOLVED FURTHER, that the Secretary is instructed to certify a copy of the Bylaws and insert the certified copy in the Record Book of the Corporation.

4. SEAL

The chair presented a Seal. The following resolution was moved, seconded and adopted:

RESOLVED, that the Seal containing the words "RTW Investments, Inc, A California Corporation" together with the date of organization of the Corporation as shown by the impression thereof on the margin of this page, is hereby adopted as the Seal of the Corporation.

5. SHARE CERTIFICATE

The chair presented a proposed form of Share Certificate to be used by the Corporation, a blank copy of which is attached to the Minutes as Exhibit "C." The following resolutions were moved, seconded and adopted:

RESOLVED, that the Share Certificate be in substantially the same form as the form of Share Certificate attached to these Minutes as Exhibit "C."

RESOLVED FURTHER, that each Share Certificate shall be consecutively numbered beginning with number 1, shall be issued only with the signature of the officers of the Corporation as provided in the Bylaws and the Seal of the Corporation affixed thereto; and

RESOLVED FURTHER, that each Share Certificate shall state the name of the Corporation, the laws of the state under which the Corporation is organized, the name of the owner to whom issued, the date of issue and number of shares represented hereby; and

RESOLVED FURTHER, that each Share Certificate shall state a statement of designations, preferences, qualifications, limitations, restrictions, and special or related rights of the holder as required under the Bylaws and the Corporations Law on the face or back of the certificate; and

RESOLVED FURTHER, that the Secretary is instructed to insert a blank Share Certificate as adopted hereby as a specimen in the Record Book of the Corporation immediately following these minutes.

6. RECORD BOOK OF THE CORPORATION

The chair stated that a book should be maintained as the Record Book of the Corporation for the purpose of collecting and having all of the important documents of the Corporation readily available. The following resolution was moved, seconded and adopted:

RESOLVED, that the Corporation shall obtain and maintain a Record Book of the Corporation, which shall include the Articles of Incorporation and any amendments thereto, and the Bylaws and any amendments thereto, the minutes of all meetings (or consents in lieu of meetings) of the Shareholders of Corporation, minutes of all meetings (or consents in lieu of meetings) of the Board of Directors of the Corporation and all other important documents.

7. OFFICERS

The chair stated that officers of the Corporation should be elected. The following resolution was moved, seconded and adopted:

RESOLVED, that the following persons are elected as officers of the Corporation to the positions set forth opposite their respective names:

OFFICE	NAME
President	Ralph Thomas Willis
Vice President	
Secretary	Ralph Thomas Willis
Chief Financial Officer/Treasurer	Ralph Thomas Willis

The Officers accepted their appointments as evidenced by their signatures on the Acceptances of Appointments by Officers attached to these Minutes.

8. PRINCIPAL PLACE OF BUSINESS IN STATE OF INCORPORATION

The chair stated that the principal place of business in the State of Incorporation of the Corporation should be identified. The following resolution was moved, seconded and adopted:

RESOLVED, that the principal place of business in the State of Incorporation of the Corporation shall be as follows:

1945 Palo Verde, Suite 101

9. AGENT FOR SERVICE OF PROCESS IN STATE OF INCORPORATION

The chair stated that the name and address of its registered agent within the State of Incorporation should be identified. The following resolution was moved, seconded and adopted:

RESOLVED, that the name and address of the registered agent of the Corporation within the State of California shall be as follows:

Name: Richard T. Williamson
Address: 1945 Palo Verde #101
Long Beach CA 90815

10. BANK RESOLUTIONS

The chair stated that a depository for the funds of Corporation is needed. The following resolutions were moved, seconded and adopted:

RESOLVED, that Ralph Thomas Willis as President of the Corporation is hereby authorized to do the following acts:

a. To designate one or more banks, trust companies, or other similar institutions as depositories of the funds, including without limitation, cash and cash equivalents of the Corporation;
b. To open, keep and close general and special bank accounts, including general deposit accounts, payroll accounts and working fund accounts with any such depository;
c. To cause to be deposited in such accounts with any such depository, from time to time, such funds, including without limitations, cash and cash equivalents of the Corporation as such officers deem necessary or advisable, and to designate or change the designation of the manager or managers, the officer or officers, and the agent or agents of the Corporation who would be authorized to make such deposits and to endorse checks, drafts or other instruments for such deposits;
d. From time to time to designate or change the designation of the officer or officers, and agent or agents of the Corporation who will be authorized to sign or countersign checks, drafts or other orders for the payment of money issued in the name of the Corporation against any funds deposited in any of such accounts, and to revoke any such designation;
e. To authorize the use of facsimile signatures for the signing or countersigning of checks, drafts or other orders for the payment of money, and to enter into such agreements as banks and trust companies customarily require as a condition for permitting the use of facsimile signatures;
f. To make such general and special rules and regulations with respect to such accounts as either of them may deem necessary or advisable; and
g. To complete and execute printed blank signature card forms in order to exercise the authority granted by this resolution, and any resolutions printed thereon shall be deemed adopted as a part hereof.

RESOLVED FURTHER, that all form resolutions required by any such depository as presented to and considered by such officers prior to the date of these minutes are hereby adopted in such forms utilized by the depository, and the Ralph Thomas Willis of the Corporation is hereby authorized to certify such resolutions as having been adopted by the Shareholders and is directed to attach such forms to these minutes as Exhibit "D" and insert the forms of such resolutions in the Record Book of the Corporation; and

RESOLVED FURTHER, that any such depository to which a copy of these resolutions, certified by the Ralph Thomas Willis of the Corporation shall have been delivered, shall be entitled to rely thereon for all purposes until it shall have received written notice of the revocation or amendment of these resolutions by the Shareholders of the Corporation.

11. PAYMENT OF EXPENSES OF ORGANIZATION

The Directors desire to reimburse costs incurred for the organization of the Corporation. The following resolution was moved, seconded and adopted:

RESOLVED, that each of the Officers of the Corporation is authorized and directed to cause Company to pay the expenses of its organization and to reimburse the persons advancing funds to the Corporation.

12. OFFER TO ISSUE SHARES

The Directors desire to offer shares for consideration. The following resolution was moved, seconded and adopted:

RESOLVED, it is deemed to be in the best interest of the Corporation to offer to sell shares to the persons and for consideration set forth below:

NAME	SHARES	CONSIDERATION

13. ISSUANCE OF SHARES

The Directors having received acceptances of their offers of shares desire to issue shares and certificates. The following resolutions were moved, seconded and adopted:

RESOLVED, that the Corporation issue the indicated shares to the persons named above in exchange for the amounts of consideration listed above;

RESOLVED FURTHER, that the officers are hereby authorized and instructed to sell and issue to the persons named above the shares indicated above upon receipt of the amounts of consideration listed; and

RESOLVED FURTHER, that the officers are authorized and directed to take all actions that may be necessary and proper for the Corporation to issue and sell the shares to the persons named, in accordance with applicable laws, and that those actions shall include, where necessary:

a. all acts that may be necessary under the federal securities laws and the securities laws of any state, including California, if advised by legal counsel preparing, verifying and filing or causing to be prepared, verified and filed on behalf of the

Corporation with the Securities and Exchange Commission five copies of a Notice of Sales of Securities (Form D) not later than fifteen (15) days after the sale and issuance of the shares described above and at such other times as are required by Rule 503 of Regulation D in order to establish the applicability of one of the exemptions provided by Regulation D for such sale and issuance; and

b. Prepare or cause to be prepared, executed and filed, with the California Commissioner of Corporations, a Notice of Transaction pursuant to Corporation Code Section 25102(f) and applicable administrative rules.

c. all acts necessary to expedite these transactions or conform them, or any of them, to the requirements of any applicable law, ruling, or regulation.

14. FEDERAL TAX MATTERS

The Directors desire to authorize actions with respect to certain tax matters. The following resolutions were moved, seconded and adopted:

FEDERAL TAX IDENTIFICATION NUMBER

RESOLVED, that the Chief Financial Officer (Treasurer) is hereby authorized and directed to complete, execute, and file or to have completed, executed and filed the Federal Form SS-4, "APPLICATION FOR EMPLOYER IDENTIFICATION NUMBER."

ADOPTION OF ACCOUNTING METHOD

RESOLVED FURTHER, that the Chief Financial Officer (Treasurer) is authorized and directed to maintain the financial records of the Corporation on the basis of the accrual method of accounting.

ADOPTION OF TAX ACCOUNTING PERIOD

RESOLVED FURTHER, that the Chief Financial Officer (Treasurer) is authorized and directed to use as the taxable year of the Corporation the tax year ending December 31.

QUALIFICATION AS SMALL BUSINESS CORPORATION

WHEREAS, this Corporation is a small business corporation, as defined in Section 1244(c)(3) of the Internal Revenue Code of 1986, as amended and Section 18151 of the California Revenue and Taxation Code; and

WHEREAS, the Corporation intends to sell and issue shares of its common stock to the persons, in the amounts and for the consideration hereinabove provided; and

WHEREAS, the consideration to be received by the Corporation for such sale and issuance will be only money or other property, other than stock or securities; and

WHEREAS, it is deemed desirable that the sale and issuance of shares of stock of the Corporation be effectuated in such a manner that qualified Shareholders may receive the benefits of Section 1244 of the Internal Revenue Code of 1986, as amended, and Section 18151 of the California Revenue and Taxation Code;

NOW, THEREFORE, BE IT RESOLVED, that the shares issued pursuant to the foregoing resolutions are intended to be "Section 1244 stock" as defined in Section 1244 of the Internal Revenue Code of 1986, as amended, and "Section 18151 stock" as defined in Section 18151 of the California Revenue and Taxation Code.

S CORPORATION ELECTION

WHEREAS, the Corporation is a domestic corporation, not a member of an affiliated group of corporations within the definition of Section 1504(a) of the Internal Revenue Code of 1986, as amended (the "Code"), nor an otherwise ineligible corporation, as defined in Sections 1361(b)(2) and (c)(6) of the Code.

WHEREAS, the Corporation does not have more than 100 shareholders, all of whom are either (1) individuals, (2) decedent's estates, (3) bankrupt's estates, or (4) trusts as specially calculated and described in Section 1361 of the Code, and none of whom are non-resident aliens or foreign trusts; and

WHEREAS, when shares of the Corporation have been sold and issued pursuant to the foregoing resolutions, this Corporation will have only one class of capital stock which is issued and outstanding; and

WHEREAS, it is deemed to be in the best interests of the Corporation and its shareholders that the corporation make an election under Subchapter S of the Internal Revenue Code, and under California Revenue and Tax Code Section 23801 to be taxed hereafter as a S Corporation pursuant to the provisions thereof;

NOW, THEREFORE, BE IT RESOLVED, that any officer of the Corporation be, and hereby is, authorized, directed and empowered on behalf of this corporation, and in its name, to execute and file with the Internal Revenue Service and the Franchise Tax Board an appropriate election on such form, instrument or document, and amendments thereto, as shall constitute an election by the Corporation to be taxed under Subchapter S of the Internal Revenue Code of 1986, as amended, and California Revenue and Tax Code Section 23801 and to do or cause to be done any and all other acts and things as such officer may, in his or her discretion, deem necessary or appropriate to carry out the purposes of the foregoing resolution, including, without limiting the generality thereof, securing the written consent to such election by each of the shareholders of the Corporation.

15. OTHER NECESSARY ACTS

The Directors desire to authorize all other acts necessary to complete the organizational process. The following resolution was moved, seconded and adopted:

RESOLVED, that each of the officers of the Corporation is authorized and directed to make such filings and applications, to execute and deliver such documents and instruments and to do such acts and obtain such licenses, authorizations, and permits as are necessary or desirable for the Corporation to conduct its business of the Corporation, to fulfill legal requirements applicable to the Corporation or its business to complete the organization of the Corporation and its qualification to do business wherever it does or desires to do business and to take any other action necessary or advisable to carry out the purposes of this resolution.

16. ADJOURNMENT

The chair asks if there is any other business before this organizational meeting of Directors. There being none, a motion to adjourn was moved, seconded and adopted and the chair declared the meeting adjourned at 11:00 a.m.

Minutes of this meeting respectfully submitted by

Dated: January 1

_____

Ralph Thomas Willis, Secretary

Appendix D

(Example)
OPERATING AGREEMENT OF
RTW INVESTMENT PROPERTIES, LLC

This Operating Agreement is entered into as of January 24, 2008, by Ralph Thomas Willis and Carl Smith referred to collectively as the Members.

A. The Members desire to form a limited liability company (Company) under the Limited Liability Company Act.
B. The Members enter into this Operating Agreement to form and provide for the governance of the Company and the conduct of its business and to specify their relative rights and obligations.

NOW, THEREFORE the terms and conditions under which the limited liability company are to be organized and operated are as follows:

SECTION I
DEFINED TERMS

The following capitalized terms shall have the meanings specified in this Section I. Other terms are defined in the text of these Regulations; and, throughout these Regulations, those terms shall have the meanings respectively ascribed to them.

"Act" means the Limited Liability Company Act, as amended from time to time.

"Regulations" means these Regulations, as amended from time to time.

"Code" means the Internal Revenue Code of 1986, as amended, or any corresponding provision of any succeeding law.

"Company" means the limited liability company organized in accordance with these Regulations.

"Comptroller" means the Comptroller of Public Accounts of the State.

"Interest" means a Person's share of the Profits and Losses of, and the right to receive distributions from, the Company.

"Interest Holder" means any Person who holds an Interest, whether as a Member or as an unadmitted assignee of a Member.

"Involuntary Withdrawal" means, with respect to RTW INVESTMENT PROPERTIES, LLC, the occurrence of any of the following events:

(i) the making of an assignment for the benefit of creditors;
(ii) the filing of a voluntary petition of bankruptcy;
(iii) the adjudication as a bankrupt or insolvent or the entry against RTW INVESTMENT PROPERTIES, LLC of an order for relief in any bankruptcy case or insolvency proceeding; or

"Member" means the Person signing these Regulations and any Person who subsequently is admitted as a member of the Company.

"Membership Rights" means all of the rights of a Member in the Company, including a Member's: (i) Interest; (ii) right to inspect the Company's books and records; (iii) right to participate in the management of and vote on matters coming before the Company; and (iv) unless these Regulations or the Articles of Organization provide to the contrary, tight to act as an agent of the Company.

"Person" means and includes an individual, corporation, partnership, association, limited liability company, or other entity, or a trust or estate.

"Profit" and "Loss" means, for each taxable year of the Company (or other period for which Profit or Loss must be computed) the Company's taxable income or loss determined in accordance with the Code.

"Transfer" means, when used as a noun, any voluntary sale, hypothecation, pledge, assignment, attachment, or other transfer, and, when used as a verb, means voluntarily to sell, hypothecate, pledge, assign, or otherwise transfer.

"Withdrawal" means a Member's dissociation from the Company by any means.

SECTION II
FORMATION AND NAME; OFFICE; PURPOSE; TERM

2.1. ORGANIZATION. Richard T. Williamson hereby organizes a limited liability company pursuant to the Act and the provisions of these Regulations and, for that purpose, has caused Articles of Organization to be prepared, executed and filed with Secretary of State to be effective on January 1, 200

2.2. NAME OF THE COMPANY. The name of the Company shall be RTW INVESTMENT PROPERTIES, LLC" The Company may do business under that name and under any other name or names agreed upon by the Members. If the Company does business under a name other than that set forth in its Articles of Organization, then the Company shall file an assumed name certificate as required by law.

2.3. PURPOSE. Company is organized to: engage in the business of the transaction of any or all lawful business for which limited liability companies may be organized under the Limited Liability Company Act; and to have all of the powers permitted by the Act, as amended from time to time.

2.4. PRINCIPAL OFFICE. The principal office of the Company in the State shall be located at:

2.5. RESIDENT AGENT. The name and address of the Company's resident agent in the State shall be:

2.6. MEMBERS. The name and present mailing address is set forth on Exhibit A.

SECTION III
MEMBERS, CAPITAL

3.1. INITIAL CAPITAL CONTRIBUTIONS. Upon the execution of these Regulations, Members shall contribute to the Company the cash and property set forth on Exhibit A and the Company shall then commence to do business.

3.2. NO OTHER CAPITAL CONTRIBUTIONS REQUIRED. No Member shall be required to contribute any additional capital to the Company, and except as set forth in the Act, no Member shall have any personal liability for any obligations of the Company.

3.3. LOANS. Any Member may, at anytime, make or cause a loan to be made to the Company in any amount and on those terms upon which the Company and the Member agree.

SECTION IV
PROFIT, LOSS, AND DISTRIBUTIONS

4.1. DISTRIBUTIONS OF CASH FLOW. Cash Flow for each taxable year of the Company shall be distributed to the Members no later than seventy-five (75) days after the end of the taxable year.

4.2. ALLOCATION OF PROFIT OR LOSS. The Profits and Losses of the Company and all items of Company income, gain, loss, deduction, or credit will be allocated, for Company book purposes and for tax purposes, to each Member in accordance with that Member's Percentage Interest.

4.3. LIQUIDATION AND DISSOLUTION. If the Company is liquidated, the assets of the Company shall be distributed to the Members in accordance with that Member's Percentage Interest.

SECTION V
MANAGEMENT: RIGHTS, POWERS, AND DUTIES

5.1. MANAGEMENT. The Company shall be managed solely by the Members

5.2. PERSONAL SERVICES. No Member shall not be required to perform services for the Company solely by virtue of being a Member. However, it is expected that the Members shall perform services and it is in consideration of these services that the Company is distributing all of its Cash Flow.

5.3. LIABILITY AND INDEMNIFICATION.

5.3.1. The Members shall not be liable, responsible, or accountable, in damages or otherwise, to the Company for any act performed by him with respect to Company matters, except for fraud.

5.3.2. The Company shall indemnify the Members for any act performed by him with respect to Company matters, except for fraud.

SECTION VI
TRANSFER OF INTERESTS AND WITHDRAWALS OF MEMBERS

6.1. TRANSFERS. Transfer of any Membership Rights requires unanimous consent of Members.

SECTION VII
DISSOLUTION, LIQUIDATION, AND TERMINATION OF THE COMPANY

7.1. EVENTS OF DISSOLUTION. The Company shall be dissolved (i) if the Members determine to dissolve the Company, or (ii) the Company has no Members for a period of ninety one (91) consecutive days. The Company shall not dissolve merely because of any one Member's Involuntary Withdrawal.

7.2. PROCEDURE FOR WINDING UP AND DISSOLUTION. If the Company is dissolved, the affairs of the Company shall be wound up. On winding up of the Company, the assets of the Company shall be distributed, first, to creditors of the Company in satisfaction of the liabilities of the Company, and then to the Persons who are the Members of the Company in proportion to their Interests.

7.3. FILING OF ARTICLES OF DISSOLUTION. If the Company is dissolved, Articles of Dissolution shall be promptly filed with the Secretary of State. If there are no remaining Members, the Articles shall be filed by the last Person to be a Member; if there are no remaining Members, or a Person who last was a Member, the Articles shall be filed by the legal or personal representatives of the Person who last was a Member.

SECTION VIII
ACCOUNTING AND TAX ELECTIONS

8.1. BANK ACCOUNTS. All funds of the Company shall be deposited in a bank account or accounts opened in the Company's name. The Members shall determine the institution or institutions at which the accounts will be opened and maintained, the types of accounts, and the Persons who will have authority with respect to the accounts and the funds therein.

8.2. ANNUAL ACCOUNTING PERIOD. The annual accounting period of the Company shall be its taxable year. The Members, subject to the requirements and limitations of the Code, shall select the Company's taxable year.

8.3. TAX ELECTION. The company will be a single member LLC and therefore taxed as a sole proprietor as a pass through entity.

SECTION IX
GENERAL PROVISIONS

9.1. ASSURANCES. The Members shall execute all such certificates and other documents and shall do all such filing, recording, publishing, and other acts as the Members deem appropriate to comply with the requirements of law for the formation and operation of the Company and to comply with any laws, rules, and regulations relating to the acquisition, operation, or holding of the property of the Company.

9.2. APPLICABLE LAW. All questions concerning the construction, validity, and interpretation of these Regulations and the performance of the obligations imposed by these Regulations shall be governed by the internal law, not the law of conflicts, of the State.

9.3. SECTION TITLES. The headings herein are inserted as a matter of convenience only, and do not define, limit, or describe the scope of these Regulations or the intent of the provisions hereof

9.4. BINDING PROVISIONS. These Regulations are binding upon, and inure to the benefit of the Members and thier heirs, executors, administrators, personal and legal representatives, Successors, and permitted assigns.

9.5. SEPARABILITY OF PROVISIONS. Each provision of these Regulations shall be considered separable; and if, for any reason, any provision or provisions herein are determined to be invalid and contrary to any existing or future law, such invalidity shall not impair the operation of or affect those portions of these Regulations which are valid.

(signature page follows)

Index

A

Active participation event, 147
Administrative burden, 48–49
Agent for service of process
 corporation, 79, 91–92, 100
 LLC, 119–21
Annual meetings, 101
Articles of incorporation
 content, 73–74
 filing requirements, 15, 47
 formalities, 73–75
Articles of organization
 filing requirements, 15, 47, 106–7, 128
 purpose, 129–30
Asset protection
 balance, 33–34
 domestic trust, 167–71
 first line of defense, 23, 25–28
 FLP benefits, 148–52
 goal, 21–22, 30
 issues, 43
 land trust, 171–72
 liability flow and, 24–25
 LLC, 124–27
 offshore plans, 173–80
 privacy issues, 44–45
 property grouping, 33–35
 second line of defense, 29
 simple approach, 32
Attorney
 contingency fee, 3
 corporation formation, 82–84, 89

LLC formation, 110–12
online formation service
 comparison, 89, 116
 referrals, 83, 112
 specialty, 84
 statistics, 2–3
Attorney-at-law, 92
Authorized stock shares, 102

B

Banking activities, 109–10
Banking authorization, 77
Barriers, 28–29
Burden of proof, 58, 59
Business-friendly states, 161–66
Business umbrella policy, 27
Buy-to-hold property. *See*
 Investor property
Buy-to-sell property. *See*
 Dealer property
Bylaws, 76, 101

C

Call the note, 119
Cardboard corporation, 81–82
C corporation
 formation, 46–47
 IRS definition, 98
 pros/cons, 12–13
 tax issues, 52, 53–54, 72, 105–6
CEO. *See* Chief executive officer
Certificate in good standing, 136

CFO. *See* Chief financial officer
Chapter C corporation.
 See C corporation
Charging order
 FLP, 150–51
 foreclosure on, 151
 LLC, 31–32
 series LLC issues, 140
Chief executive officer (CEO), 99
Chief financial officer (CFO), 99
Close corporation, 13, 98
Closely-held corporation, 98
Cloud on title, 118
Corporate compliance
 services, 94
Corporation
 advantages, 71
 agent for service of process, 79, 91–92, 100
 annual fees, 90
 annual meeting, 101
 articles of incorporation, 15, 47, 73–75
 bylaws, 101
 cardboard, 81–82
 categories, 12–13
 compliance services, 94
 Delaware incorporation, 162–64
 do-it-yourself, 87–88, 90
 FAQs, 98–102
 formation formalities, 12, 47, 73–90, 99

223

government agencies and, 93–94
hierarchy, 80–81
incorporator, 100–101
initial stock issuance, 101–2
internal documentation, 47
management, 99
Nevada incorporation, 164–66
online formation services, 84–87, 88, 89
organizational meeting, 75–78, 101
outside liabilities, 97–98
piercing corporate veil, 94–97
president, 99
privacy issues, 91
private, 98
property transfer, 92–93
public, 98
registered agent, 100
secretary, 100
S election, 78
shell, 78
state tax considerations, 64
statement of information, 79
stock, 101–2
tax ID number, 78
tax return, 90
treasurer, 99
types, 72, 98

D

DAPT. *See* Domestic asset protection trust
DBA. *See* Doing business as
Dealer property, 54–60
Debtor's hearing, 45
Deed, 118
Deep pocket assessmennt, 24
Defense barriers, 28–29
Delaware incorporation, 162–64
Developer, 55
Directors, 98
Doing business as (DBA), 46
Domestic asset protection trust (DAPT)
issues, 169–71
real estate investment and, 169
requirements, 168–69
Double taxation, 52–53
Due-on-sale clause, 93, 118–19
Due-on-transfer clause, 93, 118–19

E

EIN. *See* Employer identification number
Employer identification number (EIN), 78
Entity
administrative burden, 48–49
annual costs, 48–49
barrier, 30
choice of, 39–50
complexity level, 46–48
definition, 7
formation costs, 48
personal business needs and, 41–43
state laws affecting, 40–41
tax considerations, 51–69
tax filing requirements, 48–49
types, 7–19
separation of, 35–36
Equity shifting, 36–37
Estate of Albert Strangi v. Commissioner, 155–56
Estate of Eugene E. Stone III v. Commissioner, 157
Estate planning
succession planning, 42, 43
tax planning, 64–67, 152–54
Excess coverage policy, 27

F

Family limited partnership (FLP)
asset protection, 148–52
charging orders, 150–51
estate tax benefits, 152–54
explanation, 147–48
IRS and, 155–59
poison pill provisions, 151–52
pros/cons, 10–11
succession planning, 43
tax issues, 54
validity factors, 158
Family trust. *See* Living trust
Flip. *See* Family limited partnership
FLP. *See* Family limited partnership
Formation services, 49
Fraudulent transfer, 169, 170
Full faith and credit law, 170–71

G

General partner
entity as, 149
liability limits, 149
in limited partnership, 9
role of, 146
General partnership
complexity, 46
definition, 143
pros/cons, 8–9
Gift tax exemption, 153–54
Government agencies
corporation and, 93–94
limited liability company and, 121–22

I

Incorporation process, 80
Incorporator, 100–101
Individual ownership, 8
Inside debts, 124
Inside liability, 30–31
Insurance
landlord, 25–26
multicoverage products, 26–29
Internal Revenue Service (IRS)
C corporation, 98
dealer determination, 57–58
FLP, 155–59
Form 2553, 72, 78
offshore asset protection planning, 173–80
Schedule A, 55
Schedule C, 55
Schedule D, 55
Inter vivos trust. *See* Living trust
Investor
categories, 24–25
number of, 42

Index

property, 54–60
Irrevocable self-settled spendthrift trust, 167
Irrevocable trust, 18
IRS. *See* Internal Revenue Service
Issued stock shares, 102

J

Jointly and severally liable, 46

K

Kimball v. U.S., 157
K-1, 105

L

Landlord insurance, 25–26
Land trust, 171–72
Lawsuit protection policy, 27
Liability
   defense barriers. 28–29
   differentiating risk, 34–35
   entity barrier, 30
   flow, 21–25
   flow cap, 29
   insurance, 119
   limiting, 43
   personal risk, 46
   protection, 72
Limited liability company (LLC)
   annual meeting, 129
   articles of organization, 106–7, 128, 129–30
   asset protection, 103, 124–27
   banking activities, 109–10
   categories, 128
   charging order, 124–27
   conversion to, 130
   costs, 110–17
   dealer versus investor, 61
   disadvantages, 131
   do-it-yourself formation, 117
   FAQs, 128–31
   formation formalities, 46–47, 106–10, 128
   as general partner, 149
   government agencies and, 121–22
   inside/outside liability, 31–32
   investor ventures, 105
   membership certificates, 129
   multimember, 106, 128, 129
   name restrictions, 130–31
   online formation services, 112–17
   operating agreement, 103, 107–9, 126–30
   organizational meeting, 108–9
   organization process, 111
   ownership interests, 109
   piercing the veil, 122–24
   property transfer, 117–19, 130
   pros/cons, 15–16
   S corporation comparison, 104–5, 128
   service company use, 122
   single-member, 106, 109, 128, 129
   state tax considerations, 64
   tax issues, 54, 103, 105–6, 129
   1031 exchange, 130
   use of, 48
Limited liability limited partnership (LLLP), 12
Limited liability partnership (LLP), 11–12
Limited partner
   liability of, 9, 146–47
   outside debt consideration, 149–52
Limited partnership
   complexity, 46
   dealer versus investor, 61
   estate tax benefits, 152
   pros/cons, 9–10
   state tax considerations, 64
   structure, 146
   tax issues, 54
   uses, 143
Litigation
   age of, 1–2
   aggressive attorneys and, 2–3
   real estate investment and, 2
   society and, 3–7
Living trust, 17–18, 167
LLC. *See* Limited liability company
LLLP. *See* Limited liability limited partnership
LLP. *See* Limited liability partnership

M

Management issues, 41
Membership certificates, 129
Minutes, 75
Mortgage, due-on-sale clause, 93, 118–19
Multimember LLC, 106, 128, 129

N

Nevada incorporation, 162–64

O

Officers, 76–77, 98
Offshore asset protection plans, 173–80
Operating agreement
   creation, 103
   explanation of, 107–8, 109
   purpose of, 128, 129–30
Organizational meeting
   corporation, 75–78, 101
   limited liability company, 108–9
Outside liability
   corporation, 97–98
   example, 31–32
   limited liability company, 126

P

Partnership
   agreement, 46
   complexity, 46
   structure, 144–46
   tax issues, 54
   types, 8–12, 13
Par value, 102
Pass-through entity, 52, 53–54, 105–6
Personal assets, 34
Personal business needs, 41–43
Personal umbrella policy, 26–27
Piercing the corporate veil, 94–97
Piercing the LLC veil, 122–24

Poison pill, 151–52
Privacy issues, 43–46, 91
Private corporation, 98
Probate avoidance trust. *See*
 Living trust
Profit distributions, 41
Property
 dealer. *See* Real estate dealer
 grouping, 33–35
 investor, 55–60
 ownership, 7–19
 tax issues, 54–60, 67–69
Property transfer
 corporate issues, 92–93
 LLC issues, 117–19, 130
 requirements, 67–69
 tax consequences, 49
Public corporation, 12–13, 98

R

Real estate dealer
 court determination, 58–59
 definition, 55
 entity use, 62–63
 IRS determination, 57–58
 label avoidance, 60–63
 tax issues, 55–60
Real estate investment, 55
Reassessment issues, 67, 69
Registered agent, 100
Registered office, 100
Revised Uniform Partnership Act, 125
Revocable trust. *See* Living trust

S

S corporation
 dealer ventures, 104–5
 dealer versus investor, 61, 62–63
 formation, 46–47, 73–81
 as general partner, 149
 IRS forms, 72
 LLC comparison, 104–5, 128
 pros/cons, 14–15
 restrictions, 73
 tax issues, 53, 71–73, 98
S election form, 78
Self-employment income, 104–5
Series LLC
 in California, 137–39
 certificate in good standing, 136
 charging order issues, 140
 concept, 133
 costs, 140
 in Delaware, 133–34
 explanation, 134–39
 features, 141
 formation formalities, 139–40
 piercing the veil, 140
 pros/cons, 16–17
 statutory definition, 134
Shareholders, 98
Single-member LLC
 asset protecion, 128
 ownership interests, 109
 tax issues, 106, 129
Sole proprietorship, 46
Stock
 authorized shares, 102
 certificates, 77–78, 102
 initial issuance, 101–2
 issuance, 77–78, 102
 par value, 102
Subchapter S corporation.
 See S corporation
Subdivider, 55
Succession planning, 17, 42–43

T

Tax-deferred exchange, 57
Tax issues
 C corporation, 72
 corporate returns, 90
 dealer property versus investor property, 54–60
 entity type, 51–69
 estate tax planning, 64–67
 gift tax, 153–54
 ID number, 110
 LLC, 103, 105–6, 129
 pass-through entity, 105–6
 property tax, 67–69
 S corporation, 71–73
 state taxes, 64
1031 exchange, 56, 130
Trust
 definition, 18
 tax issues, 52, 53–54
 types, 17–18
Trustee, 44

U

ULPA. *See* Uniform Limited
 Partnership Act
Umbrella policy, 27
Uniform Limited Liability
 Company Act, 125, 137
Uniform Limited Partnership Act
 (ULPA), 125, 150
Uniform Partnership Act, 144, 145